MW00775115

20/20
Mind Sight

20/20 Mind Sight

REFOCUS, REIGNITE & REINVENT YOUR LIFE FROM THE INSIDE OUT

Rochelle,

Your presence & friendship have inspired me to rise above. I hope the gift is returned and that you enjoy the 20/20 journey of identifying & discovering even more! - Jill

Phil Fragasso & Jillian Vorce

See yourself in 20/20 focus

PW

Copyright © 2016 Phil Fragasso & Jillian Vorce
All rights reserved.

ISBN-13: 9780692709382 (Contigo Press)
ISBN-10: 069270938X

Cover design attribution: Lina Cordero-Suarez

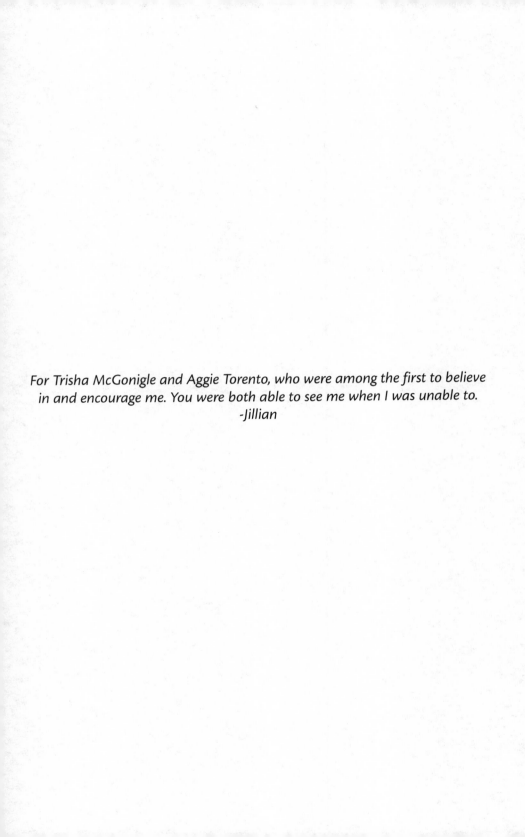

For Trisha McGonigle and Aggie Torento, who were among the first to believe in and encourage me. You were both able to see me when I was unable to.
-Jillian

Acknowledgements

M uch of this book was inspired by Phil's students at Boston College; and he is eternally grateful for their intelligence, insights, and thoughtful discourse.

There are a few people that Jillian feels compelled to acknowledge including Seth Godin, Jay Vogt, Tobe Gerard, Roy Sequeira, Rochelle Weichman, Steve Garfield, Elizabeth Weber, Larry Levine, Bruce Jones, Armandina Cueva and Lenny Lozinsky. Jillian says each of them contributed to this book either directly through shared experiences with her or indirectly by providing encouragement and inspiration. In her words, "Truthfully, each person I have met has in some way contributed to this book. Experience, relationships, and confidence are all cumulative and interconnected."

Table of Contents

"I Should Have Been More Specific"

"People are idiots" is one of Phil's most common riffs. As pejorative as it sounds, he always meant it to suggest that people should think for themselves and take the advice and opinions of others with a huge grain of salt. So you can imagine his delight when Soledad O'Brien, the CNN journalist, gave the same bit of advice to the Harvard University Class of 2013. Her exact phrasing was, "People are idiots and you shouldn't listen."

It's such simple advice and yet so difficult for most people to follow. We've been taught to listen to our elders and "do as I say." And while most advice is offered with the genuine desire to be helpful, it's usually without context or a full understanding of the life, skills, and aspirations of the receiving party. We each see life through our own filters, so the advice we offer flows through those same filters.

The only advice that truly matters is the advice we provide ourselves. The effectiveness of that advice is contingent on our degree of self-knowledge and is in direct proportion to the amount of time and energy we devote to personal reflection. We can't know what advice is appropriate for ourselves until we truly know who we are and what we hold most important.

The only advice Ms. O'Brien provided the Harvard graduates was to develop a personal mindset that will lead to personal fulfillment: "Figure out your dream and be brave enough to go and live it. Otherwise, someone will hire you to go ahead and help them with their dream."

Have You Thought Today?

An MBA student recounted this job-hunting story as part of a "Personal Assessment" assignment:

> I had strong interviews with the CFO and controller. They both assured me that I would be hired. The final interview with the CEO seemed a mere formality. However, the CEO challenged me with questions I had never been asked before: what my personal brand was, what specific skills differentiated me from my peers, where I envisioned myself professionally in the short and long-term, and how I planned to achieve those goals. Fumbling over my words and regurgitating my professional strengths, I could sense that I was unable to adequately answer these basic questions. I found out three days later that I didn't get the job. While I was heartbroken, I found myself more troubled by the fact that not only could I not articulate my personal and professional brand, I had not even thought of it.

This student's story is a common one. Very few people give a moment's thought to who they are, what they believe, what they stand for, how they're perceived, and what they want to achieve.

It's easy to blame the educational system and its focus on the regurgitation of facts and figures rather than a reflection of the interplay of all the components of modern life. Similarly, it's easy to blame the business world for training employees to do as told and play nice in the corporate sandbox. And it's equally easy to point a finger at parents who preached, "You can be whatever you want to be" but never gave their children the time or insight to figure out exactly what that might be. The focus in school, in business, and at home has long been on the endgame – i.e., an impressive-sounding response to the common cocktail party query: "So what do you do?"

The response to "What do you do?" pales in comparison to such queries as "Who are you?" "What do you want to do with your life?" And "Why do you want to do it?" Unfortunately, few people ask the latter type of questions. The blame for that falls squarely on the individual. Yes, your parents, teachers, and bosses may have avoided the subject for a thousand different reasons; but you ignore it at your own peril. You ignore it at the risk of living a life that is not just unfulfilling but, far worse, is a shallow and meaningless lie.

The simplest solution is to think for oneself. Thinking, after all, is what truly distinguishes humans from every other species. Why then do so few of us do it? And *yes*, we are suggesting that the majority of people spend little time actually thinking in the fullest sense of the word. Thinking does not mean wondering, evaluating, choosing, affirming, or denying. It often comprises some or all of those activities, but true thinking goes much deeper and does not content itself with superficial musings.

Thinking is simple, but it's also one of the hardest – and sometimes most terrifying – things we do. Understanding the factors that make it so hard is a key theme throughout the book. If you question why thinking is so important, consider this quote from the Irish author George Bernard Shaw: "Few people think more than two or three times a year. I've made an international reputation for myself by thinking once or twice a week."

Welcome To *20/20 Mind Sight*

20/20 Mind Sight has grown out of our combined experiences as corporate executives, consultants, educators, coaches, and thought leaders. We've written the kind of book we wish we could have read when we first started out in our adult lives and a book we would still find useful today after achieving far more than we could ever have envisioned. We attribute our success and worldview to an education and a mindset steeped in reflection – both internal and external. It's a mindset that should be far more common, and a mindset that can help transform "hammer heads" who view everything as a nail into "monkey wrenches" who are not afraid to ask probing questions in order to discover the truth, the whole truth, and nothing but the truth.

The book combines real-life examples (both contemporary and historical), anecdotes, worksheets, questionnaires, and online tools designed to help identify and create a distinctive mindset that can lead to new levels of personal satisfaction and success. That mindset has been bowdlerized and watered down in literally hundreds of books promoting quick-fix paths to leadership, wealth, power, love, influence, career success, and powerful personal brands. The problem is that most of the "tips" are focused on *doing* rather than *thinking*. Indeed, in many cases, what's delivered is a crass and manipulative message that fails to inspire breakthrough insights or affect the reader's life in any meaningful way. That's the key differentiator of our book.

Think about it from this perspective. Most people fall into jobs that turn into careers that turn into a lifetime of work that's unchallenging, unfulfilling and, in far too many cases, unsuited to the individual's strengths, interests, and aspirations. The key question is how could this happen in an age of total transparency when information on any topic is easily accessible in any language and at any time of day or night. The reason is that far too much time and energy are focused on job titles, career ladders, and the holy grail of capitalism: a big paycheck that's the envy of family, friends, and foes. Conversely, far too little time is spent thinking about what's truly important to the individual. More specifically and most importantly, almost no time is spent considering what is of critical importance to the innermost character and passion of the individual. Lily Tomlin said, "I always wanted to be somebody, but I should have been more specific." Her remark speaks to the primary benefit of building a 20/20 mindset.

From Theory to Practice: 20/20 Sight Lines

To make the content as engaging and long-lasting as possible, we're introducing a wide range of tools, surveys, and questionnaires to help the reader gauge his or her mastery of the issue. In some cases an in-text questionnaire is included, and in others the reader will be referred to a web link (usually hosted by an educational entity or a non-profit organization). These tools include:

- Johari Window
- Nohari Window
- Jungian Typology
- Implicit Association Test
- Satisfaction with Life Scale

- The Grit Survey
- Locus of Control

"The privilege of a lifetime is being who you are."

Every Journey Starts Somewhere

While not designed specifically to help the reader climb the corporate ladder or generate wealth beyond anyone's wildest dreams, the process of building a 20/20 mindset will unquestionably lead to new heights and distant places.

Joseph Campbell, the American mythologist, observed that, "The privilege of a lifetime is being who you are." Campbell understood that life is both a process of continual discovery and an ever-changing destination. We trust *20/20 Mind Sight* will help readers begin the journey.

CHAPTER 1: *"WHAT THE HELL IS WATER?"*

Put The "I" In You

I n his now-classic commencement speech to Kenyon College's class of 2005, David Foster Wallace tells the story of two young fish who are swimming along when they happen upon an older fish who greets them and asks, "How's the water?" The two young fish swim on in silence for a bit until one of them turns to the other and asks, "What the hell is water?" The point of the story as Wallace explains is that our "most obvious, ubiquitous, important realities are often the ones that are the hardest to see and talk about." Like the fish in Wallace's story, many people choose – consciously or subconsciously – to lie to themselves, create alternate realities, and live unmanaged, meandering lives.

For most people, there's a huge disconnect between perception and reality. Who we think we are often differs substantially from who we really are. Our perception of how we're viewed by others often conflicts with the reality of how others see us. All of this is because our personal beliefs and characteristics have not been fully tested or vetted. We accept superficial affirmations that we're good people, attractive, kind and intelligent. We rarely question our assumptions. We fall victim to unacknowledged biases. We're not who we think we are or who we want to become. Instead, we define ourselves as the outside world – friends, colleagues, bosses, subordinates, teachers, and loved ones – has taught us to be. At its most extreme, we take a backseat role in our own lives content to let others pull our strings and write our life scripts.

Please reread the preceding paragraph and pay particular attention to the last two sentences. Much of what we believe about ourselves – ranging from our strengths and triumphs to our weaknesses and failures – results from looking into the mirror that the outside world has held up for us. But just as a funhouse mirror distorts our physical appearance, this externally generated mirror distorts our psyche in the fullest sense of the term: i.e., the spiritual, emotional, and motivational aspects of the mind.

The primary objective in creating a 20/20 mindset is to smash that externally generated mirror and allow our psyche to flourish in a way that achieves maximum personal satisfaction and delivers maximum value to the people, organizations, and world around us. Aristotle said, "Knowing yourself is the beginning of all wisdom." He further stated that the ability to harness and utilize that wisdom provides the springboard to a life of happiness.

Perhaps most importantly, a 20/20 approach to life provides a doorway to self-love. Think about the people you love. In all likelihood you came to love them by learning about their beliefs, aspirations, likes and dislikes, core values, and passions. It works the same with each of us: *we come to love ourselves only by learning about ourselves.*

Be Honest With Yourself And Others

There is one place where frank recognition of who we are and unabashed admission of the life we lead is the norm rather than the exception. That place is Alcoholics Anonymous.

"Hello. My name is John and I'm an alcoholic."

That's the traditional introduction used at AA meetings. It's a simple and powerful message with both emotional and literal implications. Recognizing themselves as alcoholics is something that AA members live with every day of their lives. It guides their actions and beliefs. It's who they are.

None of this is meant to imply that alcoholics don't have other attributes. They might be loving husbands or mothers, skilled nurses or architects, gifted artists or athletes. None of us are only one thing. Humans are complex organisms with strengths and weaknesses – some of which we recognize, some that we ignore, and some that remain invisible to the day we die. Most AA members have taken long and painful journeys before being able to recognize and confront their alcoholism. In a very real sense, it's the formal recognition of their addiction that allows them to continue their life's journey and make the most of every day and every interaction with loved ones, friends and colleagues.

All of us also have a life's journey that can be dramatically enhanced by recognizing and embracing who we are at our core. If you were asked to introduce yourself using the same rubric as an AA meeting, what would you say? Something like this?

"Hello. My name is John and I'm a lawyer."

"Hello. My name is Susan and I'm a devoted mother and wife."

Or perhaps you'd go out on a limb and describe yourself like this:

"Hello. My name is Anna and I'm a doctor by day and an aspiring writer by night."

"Hello. My name is Bill and I'm an accountant who wishes he were a park ranger."

Or maybe you're a truly wild-and-crazy guy or gal who says this:

"Hello. My name is Kevin and I'm halfway through my life's journey, still trying to find my way."

"Hello. My name is Carol and I'm exactly what you see."

None of these examples comes close to the impact and honesty of the AA introduction. The first four provide functional labels, while the last two deliver vague, hip-sounding platitudes designed to end the conversation before anyone probes too deeply.

The reason so many of us have difficulty with this kind of exercise is that we don't really know ourselves. Alfred Adler, the Austrian psychotherapist who broke away from Sigmund Freud to found his own school of individual psychology, believed this: "The hardest thing for human beings to do is to know themselves and to change themselves." That profoundly simple statement gets to the core of what *20/20 Mind Sight* is all about.

> **"The hardest thing for human beings to do is to know themselves and to change themselves."**

The Key Question

Phil often asks his undergraduate students to name the one person they never want to disappoint. The typical answer is "my parents." The more

PHIL FRAGASSO & JILLIAN VORCE

daring and astute offer "myself." The correct answer, from our perspective at least, is "my future self." It's your future self who will look back and evaluate the decisions you make, the people you love and befriend, the work you do, and the difference you make in the world around you. We can think of no greater sadness than lying on one's deathbed filled with regret and self-reproach. Yet that happens more often than not because we tend to make life choices that are easy and expedient. We ignore future ramifications, try not to make waves, and embrace complacency over transformation. It's easier to say yes and go along with the crowd than to say no and follow your own path. And it's far easier to do what someone else tells you to do than determine your own goals and priorities.

Everything we achieve in life begins with ourselves. That goes for whether we measure achievement by personal satisfaction and happiness or wealth and fame. Most people spend little time on self-reflection and instead rely too much on the direction provided by others. The American mythologist Joseph Campbell stated it like this:

> **"The world is full of people who have stopped listening to themselves or have listened only to their neighbors to learn what they ought to do, how they ought to behave, and what the values are that they should be living."**

As important as it is to have a cadre of people from whom you can request advice and counsel, there is a fine line between friendly suggestion and deliberate manipulation. That line is increasingly being crossed.

True power and fulfillment come from self-knowledge, but knowing yourself is just the beginning. "History's great achievers – Napoleon, da Vinci, Mozart – have always managed themselves," said Peter Drucker. And that, he continued, "is what makes them great achievers."

The Curse of Personality

The cultural historian Warren Susman observed that we, as a society, have shifted from a focus on character to an obsession with personality. Prof. Susman passed away in 1985 – long before "big-personalities" like the

Kardashians, Snooki, and Honey Boo-Boo began to dominate the television airways and publicity-crazed politicians like Ted Cruz hijacked Congress – but his words have never been truer or more discouraging. The pervasive tendency to focus on what we say and how we act in public rather than how we behave in private is a major contributing factor to the general lack of personal reflection and self-knowledge.

More value is placed on how we're perceived than who we actually are. In a very real sense, we're falling victim to the marketing aphorism to "sell the sizzle not the steak." It doesn't matter how good the steak actually is. What matters is getting the customer to buy the steak based on the marketer's unabashed manipulation. Susman lamented that our social role was increasingly being defined as a "performer." We were performing for someone else's benefit rather than our own edification. We sacrifice personal growth and understanding for a few moments of public approbation.

An often quoted adage in the business world is that you can't manage what you can't measure. A similar truism exists for our personal lives: "you can't change what you don't acknowledge." A focus on personality rather than character is a refusal, conscious or not, to acknowledge our inner workings.

As with most journeys, the act of recognizing and acknowledging one's core character is the first and arguably the most important step in building a life of happiness and fulfillment. The first "20/20 Sight Line" exercise will help you accomplish that.

20/20 Sight Line: The Johari Window

On a daily basis we deal with three conflicting realities about ourselves:

- The You as you see yourself
- The You as you're seen by others
- The You as you want to be seen by others

The Johari Window is a psychological tool developed in 1955 and named for its inventors, Joseph Luft and Harry Ingham. It provides a useful model to explore the interplay among our various interpersonal realities and gain insight into how we see ourselves versus how others see us.

The Johari Window distinguishes between what you know and don't know about yourself, and what others know or don't know about you. It then plots the overlaps, inconsistencies, and gaps into a four-paned "window" as depicted in the accompanying graphic. Each of the four window "panes" provides insight into a specific aspect of our communications and relationship-building behaviors.

THE JOHARI WINDOW

	Known To Self	Unknown To Self
Known To Others	**OPEN** My Public Self	**BLIND** My Blind Spots
Unknown To Others	**HIDDEN** My Hidden Self	**UNKNOWN** My Unconscious Self

- *Open* -- This quadrant reflects your "public self" and includes "open" topics that are presented and observed with honesty and little defensiveness.
- *Blind* -- Think of this as the "spinach in the tooth" quadrant. Interpersonal communication in this pane tends to be hesitant and circumspect because others aren't quite sure what you know or don't know. Your goal is to make this pane the smallest of the quadrants.
- *Hidden* -- If you have a skeleton in your closet, it lives here. To some extent, you control the flow of communication regarding information in this quadrant and share personal details only as circumstances and comfort levels dictate.
- *Unknown* -- This is the province of Freud and Jung where the unconscious reigns supreme. We don't know what we don't know and neither do the people we associate with.

The Johari Window provides an opportunity to better align the realities, perceptions, and aspirations of your inner self -- and better experience yourself as others do.

As a self-actualization tool, the Johari Window is quite easy to use. We strongly recommend that you create your Johari baseline profile and then invite at least a dozen friends, colleagues, and family members to provide their own input. The feedback will move you one step closer to recognizing and understanding the actual "I" that resides in "You."

Access the Johari Window exercise via this link: **20-20MindSight.com/ chapter1**

Extra Credit

The only criticism we've ever heard about the Johari Window is that it only includes positive traits. If you're willing to run the risk of a walk on the wild side, you can also check out Nohari's evil twin: the Nohari Window. You can access this exercise with the same link:

20-20MindSight.com/chapter1

CHAPTER 2: *"THE YEARS ARE SHORT"*

Find Your Passion

The job-search website Monster.com ran a powerful and jarring television ad during the 1999 Super Bowl. Filmed starkly in black-and-white, the ad featured children delivering these lines in simultaneously humorous and disturbing tones:

When I grow up, I want to file all day.
I want to claw my way up to middle management.
Be replaced on a whim.
I want to have a brown nose.
I want to be a yes man.
Yes woman.
Yes sir. Coming sir.
Anything for a raise sir.
When I grow up ...
When I grow up ...
I want to be under-appreciated.
Be paid less for doing the same job.
I want to be forced into early retirement.

The ad ends with a voiceover asking, "What do you want to be?" The commercial resonated with viewers because it forces us to face the facts of our existence, ugly as they may be. It dares us to compare our dreams and aspirations to the realities of our day-to-day lives. No one wants to grow up to be a Yes-Man or Yes-Woman. No one aspires to be under-appreciated and underpaid. People would never want any of this to happen to them, yet it happens all the time. Look around your office, your school, and your community. The odds are that the people who are operating and contributing below their potential far outnumber those who are truly satisfied and fulfilled peak performers. While you're looking around, consider which group you're in – the under-performers or the peak performers. Most importantly, ask yourself whether this is the life and career you envisioned when you were young. If not, there's still time to change.

Got Passion?

Ask young children what they want to be when they grow up and you'll usually see their faces burst with smiles as they imagine a future as a doctor, rock star or fireman. Their parents also smile as their kids indulge their personal fantasies. As the children grow older, however, and enter adolescence and young adulthood, parents are not always quite so amused and supportive of their kids' desire to follow their passion. Even the most well-meaning parents harbor deep-seated ambitions and judgments about their children's career choices. A six-year-old who wants to be a hip-hop dancer is considered cute; a twenty-year-old with the same dream is considered delusional. Young people are regularly discouraged from pursuing careers deemed impractical, unseemly, or insufficiently remunerative. Sometimes the culprits are family, friends, or teachers; but sometimes the discouragement bubbles up from inside. We have a natural fear of failure, but that fear is exacerbated when the threat of failure springs from something we're passionate about. In some cases we won't even give voice to our passions because success seems too remote or improbable. This suppressed passion is often the root cause of the unhappiness, restlessness, and dissatisfaction that distinguishes far too many lives.

Impassioned vs. Indentured

If you're like most people, the romantic pursuit of your spouse or significant-other represents the most impassioned activity of your life. You probably spent years dating potential candidates and kissing far too many frogs before you came upon "The One." You met him or her and then focused all your attention on building a loving relationship that was mutual and long-lasting.

Is that how you chose your job? Did you know what you were looking for, turn over a lot of rocks in the process, and finally identity the one position in the one company that would satisfy everything you wanted in a job? If you're nodding, you're probably also lying. Most people fall into their first jobs haphazardly. They might have had a buddy who worked at the particular firm, their uncle's sister-in-law had a contact there, or they stumbled upon that particular company's booth at a recruiting fair.

Occasionally the job you stumble upon is a perfect match but more often it's like forcing the proverbial square peg into a round hole. While it's true that opposites can indeed fall in love and live happily ever after in our personal lives, it's not at all true in our work lives. We spend more time at work than we do with our families and friends, so it should be work that we love and are passionate about. Otherwise, you ought to keep kissing additional frogs until you fall in love with a prince of a company and a position that makes you feel more like royalty than a serf.

Passion Is Job One

The most common question asked of business leaders is this: "What keeps you up at night?" A more appropriate question is, "What gets you up in the morning." High achievers understand, "The days are long, but the years are short," so they focus on making every day and every year count – and continually move towards achieving their lifetime vision. In the recent patent infringement trial between Apple and Samsung, Christopher Stringer, one of Apple's most senior designers, explained his department's mission to the jury like this: "Our role is to imagine products that don't exist and guide them to life." That is an unequivocally inspired approach to work and a compelling reason to get up every morning.

"The days are long, but the years are short."

Passion cannot be faked. It's not something you can learn or emulate. It's a positive vibe, flow, or mojo that bubbles up from the inside and casts a radiant glow on all we see and do. Our passions are unique and discovering them is critical to living a life of fulfillment and happiness. The philosopher William James wrote, "I have often thought that the best way to define a man's character would be to seek out the particular mental or moral attitude in which, when it came upon him, he felt himself most deeply and intensively active and alive. At such moments, there is a voice inside which speaks and says, *this is the real me!*" President Clinton discovered that voice and his passion for politics early in his life. His career was notable for incredible highs and lows, yet he often said, "I love my job on the worst of days."

Along similar lines, Mark Twain rightly observed that, "Thousands of geniuses live and die undiscovered – either by themselves or by others." You needn't be one of them.

> *"Thousands of geniuses live and die undiscovered*
> *– either by themselves or by others."*

The Routine Of Passion

Ray Allen made more three-point shots than anyone in NBA history. Anyone who has seen Allen play swears the guy is a natural. He's focused, his release is silky smooth, and the arc of the ball is pure magic. Put it all together and it looks like he's hardly trying; but that's actually the result of his passion for the game and trying so hard to get it perfect. Allen is one of the most diligent and disciplined athletes in the NBA or any other sport. He gets to the locker room three hours before tip-off and shoots hundreds of balls, all by himself. He's the quintessential team player, but he understands that the best way to help his team is to keep improving his own skills. Part of that improvement is the routine.

It sounds counter-intuitive but routines are often the driving force behind personal achievement. Notwithstanding the common belief that routines are evidence of a dull and dreary mindset, they are actually quite the opposite. Routines are a manifestation of one's passion. Routines get you in the game. They focus all your energy on the goal. In truth, they're somewhat Pavlovian because they operate at a subconscious level. They feed your passion and drive your success.

Think about your own passion and the routines that support it. If you don't have a passion-building routine, get one. It's part of being the best you can be and living a life of meaning and fulfillment.

The Passionate Route To Happiness And Success

Pursuing a career or avocation that you are passionate about is the single most effective way to ensure personal and professional happiness. It makes sense. The more excited you are by an endeavor and the more it stretches and challenges you, the harder you're going to work to succeed at it. You won't be going through the motions; you'll be focused and energized. It will be fun. Thomas Edison stated it perfectly: "I never did a day's work in my life. It was all fun."

It doesn't matter what career you pursue; it's what that career means to you. How it speaks to you and the personal need it satisfies. We all know lawyers who hate their jobs and others who love what they do. The same goes for nurses, salespeople, educators, carpenters, florists, and economists. Two people can have the exact same job working with the exact same people in the same building and come away with two diametrically opposed perspectives. One might feel drained just getting up in the morning and preparing to go to work, while the other can't wait to – in the eloquent words of the always-impassioned management guru Tom Peters – "Do cool shit. Every damn day." In fact, make that your mantra. Your Holy Grail. Your life's work.

"Do cool shit. Every damn day."

20/20 Sight Line: The Jung Typology Test

Discovering your passion is an intensely personal activity. Nonetheless, there are some tools that use self-reflection to assess where your passions lie and perhaps help nudge you in the right direction.

The Myers-Briggs Type Indicator (MBTI) is the most widely used measure of personality types. The MBTI methodology is based on the work of Carl Jung, and MBTI questionnaires are typically administered by specially trained consultants. That makes MBTI testing cost-prohibitive for individuals. As a starting point, however, Humanmetrics Inc. offers a free online testing program – "The Jung Typology Test." Phil has used this program with MBA students and can confirm that the results are highly correlated to MBTI results.

Upon completion of the Humanmetrics questionnaire, you will:

- Obtain your 4-letter type formula according to the typology developed by Carl Jung and Isabel Briggs Myers, along with the strengths of preferences and the description of your personality type
- Discover careers and occupations most suitable for your personality type
- See which famous personalities share your type
- Access free career development resources

Without replicating all of the information readily available about the Jungian and Myers-Briggs analyses, here's the nutshell version. Human consciousness is characterized by four personality dimensions:

- Extraversion vs. Introversion
- Sensing vs. Intuition
- Thinking vs. Feeling
- Judging vs. Perceiving

Within each of these dichotomies, people typically have a preference of one trait/approach over the other (e.g., a greater tendency to think rather than feel when making decisions). This preference can range from mild to extensive.

The possible permutations of the four dichotomies yield the 16 different combinations (different personality types) shown here:

ISTJ	ISFJ	INFJ	INTJ
ISTP	ISFP	INFP	INTP
ESTP	ESFP	ENFP	ENTP
ESTJ	ESFJ	ENFJ	ENTJ

Access the Jung Typology Test via this link: **20-20MindSight.com/chapter2**

NOTE: Some of this information is used with the permission of Humanmetrics Inc. The Humanmetrics Jung Typology Test™ instrument uses methodology, questionnaire, scoring and software that are proprietary to Humanmetrics Inc., and should not be confused with the MBTI®, Myers-Briggs®, and/or Myers-Briggs Type Indicator® instrument."

CHAPTER 3: *"IF GOD LIVED ON EARTH"*

Take Off the Blinders

The "Standpoint Theory," introduced by German philosopher Georg Hegel, states that people's experiences, knowledge, and opinions are shaped by the social groups to which they belong. Taken together these perspectives create a worldview that is unique to each of us. The resulting "standpoint" determines what we focus on, what we obscure, and what we are truly blind to. The American philosopher, William James, complemented Hegel by arguing that human beings were blind "to the feelings of creatures and people different from ourselves." It is this very blindness that, if left unchecked, can progress from a simple preference for similar-looking people to surface-level stereotypes to the dangerous social pathology of full-blown racism.

A fully realized 20/20 mindset helps individuals remove their prejudicial blinders by acknowledging their presence. Everyone is prejudiced to some degree. We may suppress those feelings from being outwardly expressed, or we may even deny them to ourselves. The key is to turn off the various personal filters that cloud judgment and focus instead on accepting other people's realities. Acknowledge the differences and then accept, embrace and appreciate them.

The key tenets of *20/20 Mind Sight* are personal reflection and self-knowledge. Their importance to the concept of a blinders-free perspective cannot be overstated. People who truly know themselves and feel comfortable in their own skin tend to be the most open-minded – i.e., the most impartial and least judgmental. They are confident about their own values and beliefs and, as a direct result, do not feel compelled to force those values and beliefs on others. On the other hand, people who have not yet delved deep inside to test and question their beliefs and values are far more likely to fear and denigrate the mass of others who do not look, sound, or act exactly like they do. These less reflective individuals are driven to persuade the "others" to accept and validate their own worldview. It's "my way or the highway" for those whose self-knowledge is constrained by ideology and indoctrination – as well as a lack of general curiosity and appreciation for the world at large. Their life's journey consists of a single track in the shape of a circle. They go round and round seeing the same things over and over again. The more they see those same things, the more partial they become towards them.

Be Partial To Your Impartialities

Ironically, the political correctness of today's world contributes to the difficulty of accepting our own prejudices. We're so afraid of hurting someone's feelings or giving the slightest suggestion that we are biased for or against some group of people that we stifle even the most innocuous comments.

Consider this example. When Phil asks his students to complete the sentence, "Irish people like to _____," they all chuckle and shout out "drink." Then when he asks, "Asians are _____," they laugh and say "good at math" or "bad drivers." A moment later, when he asks them to complete the sentence, "Black people like to eat_____," they all freeze. No one speaks. Most bow their heads and avert their eyes. Then when Phil suggests "watermelon" or "fried chicken" as possible answers they almost gasp in unison. Why? Because they have the mistaken belief that speaking the words aloud means they condone racism. And when Phil asks them why it's okay to suggest the Irish like to drink and Asians are poor drivers – both of which are just as stereotypical and far more derogatory – they don't know. It just *seems* to them that the Irish and Asian stereotypes are amusing while the Black stereotype is demeaning.

Just as interestingly, when there are Black students in the class, they will immediately shout out "fried chicken." They think it's funny the same way the Irish students think it's funny to be thought of as heavy drinkers. But somehow it's different. Perhaps it's due to political correctness. Perhaps it's an indication of White guilt for the horrors of slavery, Jim Crow and Selma.

Or perhaps there is some deep-seated bias that exists within us even as we struggle to contain it.

Different Doesn't Mean Better Or Worse

There's a Yiddish proverb that suggests, "If God lived on earth, people would break his windows." The point is that even the ideals that live in our minds would not survive the harsh light of reality.

Consider the likely response if Jesus suddenly appeared in the twenty-first century in the exact human form He embodied in Jerusalem. How many people do you honestly think would accept His divinity, sing His praises, and offer adulation? As you're thinking about your own response to a modern-day Jesus, remember that He'd probably be around five feet tall, the average height for that time. He'd probably look more like Saddam Hussein than the blue-eyed, sandy-haired Adonis pictured in prayer books, paintings, and religious magazines. And, if He remained true to His teachings, He would look with love upon all men and women regardless of race, sexual orientation, or political beliefs. He'd also shower love upon the adherents of any and all non-Christian religions. He would fully understand that very few people choose a specific religion on their own – they simply adopt the religion of their family. He would understand that even the most fervent Catholics and most devoted Muslims would likely be impassioned Jews if they'd been born into a Jewish family.

This modern-day Jesus would ask how could anyone hate or scorn or commit violence against someone whose only "crime" was following in their parents' footsteps? Those footsteps will likely be different than the path your own parents took, but different is not a judgmental term. Different just means different – not better or worse. That understanding – simple yet profound – provides the bedrock to a lifetime journey on an impartial path to human compassion, love, and understanding.

It's Sometimes Okay To Be Politically Incorrect

As a straight white male, Phil hasn't had to deal with overt prejudice or knee-jerk stereotyping. Jillian, however, is a young, openly gay woman. (*Hi, it's Phil here. I have to add that Jillian is also a beautiful and charismatic woman. That means she often gets hit on by men who sometimes don't accept "no" or "gay" as her final answer.)* Here's a perspective on how to effectively communicate with "different" people in Jillian's own words.

> Most people have a visceral fear of saying the wrong thing. They don't want to sound offensive or be judged negatively. Taken together those concerns stop many people from asking the kind of questions that would add genuine insight into the other's world. As a result, meaningful dialogue is rare. The sad irony is that this lack of dialogue and open communication serves to deepen the chasm that separates people. In a very real sense silence feeds and festers the misunderstanding, ignorance, distrust, and aversion that typify bias and discrimination.
>
> When people ask me about being gay, they are almost always politically incorrect. Their words and approach, in most cases, could easily be considered rude and/or inappropriate. But that's okay. I instead focus on their intent. And because so many people won't allow themselves to ask questions, I greatly respect when someone takes that first step.
>
> I'm not a martyr by any means, so before I engage with someone I do try to gauge whether they're coming from a place of genuine curiosity. The good news is the vast majority of people are authentic. So I try to be as well. I never claim to speak for the entire LGBT community. I simply speak openly about my own experience and don't allow myself to become bothered or frazzled by any unsettling phraseology on the questioner's part. If they inquire with an open mind, then I need to respond in kind.
>
> It all sounds so simplistic when I put these words on paper. Of course I would engage with people who want to engage with me. Of course I would speak openly when someone speaks openly to me. To do otherwise would be to abdicate what I believe is my core responsibility as a member of the human race – to connect with others to improve all of our lives.

The moral of the story is that we can never truly understand "others" until we interact with them. Observation from a safe distance will never allow us to dive under the superficial differences that separate us. Move closer, phrase your question as well as you can, and prepare to be surprised and delighted.

42 Yesterday And Today

The 2013 Jackie Robinson biopic 42 includes a gut-wrenching, cinematic stab to the heart. The Dodgers were playing in Cincinnati for the first time with Jackie Robinson as a member of the team. The camera was focused on a young boy who was thrilled to be attending his first major league game. His dad was telling him about his own first game when Robinson stepped onto the field amid a torrent of vitriol and racial epithets. The boy's father shouted out his own racist taunts as the boy looked back and forth from his dad's face to Robinson. A few moments later, the boy joined in and began shouting similar invectives at Robinson. His indoctrination as an unthinking racist had began.

A few moments later, Dodger shortstop Pee Wee Reese went over to comfort Robinson. He put his arm around his new teammate and thanked him. "For what?" Robinson asked. Reese looked up into the stands and said that he was from Louisville and a lot of his friends and family were at the game – and he wanted them to know the kind of man he was and what he stood for. They wouldn't like him consorting with a black man but that was too damn bad.

In the case of Pee Wee Reese, the indoctrination hadn't worked; but he was a rare exception. He would still be one today. Very few of us can withstand and grow beyond the implicit and explicit prejudices that get pounded into our heads. Our parents, friends, churches, schools, and workplaces are often part of the problem. The only true solution is personal reflection and self-knowledge.

The only reason anyone could hate Jackie Robinson was that they were taught to hate. Indeed, they were encouraged to hate. Some sixty-something years later, young people are still being taught to hate people who are different -- whether the differences are based on skin color, religion, gender, sexual preference, or a host of other social, economic and political factors.

The Unequivocal *Why* In The Boston Marathon Bombings

Immediately after the arrest of Dzhokhar Tsarnaev, the surviving perpetrator of the Boston Marathon bombing of 2013, the focus of law enforcement and the media switched to questions of *why*. What could possibly have caused two seemingly normal and assimilated young men to turn into senseless killers? The focus, as always, was the search for a specific cause ranging from Islamic jihad to ethno-centric separatism to political/social injustice to religious repression/fanaticism.

Whatever the "specific" cause, the root cause was unequivocally indoctrination followed by blind faith to a person, organization, or orthodoxy. Blind faith refers to beliefs that are held without true understanding, reasoned discrimination, or experiential proof. While an argument can be made that all faith is blind by definition, for our purpose we'll focus on the articles of faith that serve to dehumanize and engender hate.

Take a moment to consider your most deeply held beliefs, and then focus on those that originated from an external source. The beliefs you hold because you were taught to hold them. Examples might include the belief that women are subservient (and belong in the kitchen and out of the boardroom), homosexuality is an abomination (and gay marriage will destroy traditional marriage), Muslims are terrorists (and shouldn't be allowed to build mosques in "our" neighborhood), Jews are stingy and greedy (and plotting to take over the world), and Mexicans are lazy (and so we have to build an electrified fence on our southern border to keep them out and stop them from taking our jobs). No one – and we truly mean no one – ever derived these beliefs on his or her own. They are the result of indoctrination by one or more of the groups we belong to (family, school, church, civic, etc.) and the lack of a questioning mindset of our own.

Our educational, corporate and community institutions have trained us to repeat and regurgitate. Introspection and personal reflection are unvalued, ignored, discouraged or – in extreme cases – punished. We've become a society of blind followers with little insight into our personal character, and we all suffer as a result. That's why the "lives of quiet desperation" that Thoreau described are so prevalent and why civil discourse has been replaced with the coarse language of divisiveness and disdain.

Few of us take this blind faith to the extreme of the two Marathon bombers, but we all suffer from it. The good news is we can overcome it with a modicum of personal reflection and self-knowledge.

Are You Partial To Your Friends?

One of the most powerful exercises Phil uses in class is to have the students write down the names of their three closest friends. He then asks them to draw three columns next to those names and put a checkmark in the first column for each of those people who are a different race than themselves. A checkmark goes in the second column if any of them practice a different religion; and a checkmark goes in the third column if any of them have a different sexual orientation. Phil ends the exercise by asking how many checkmarks they have. Try it for yourself:

Name	Different race	Different religion	Different sexual orientation

In a typical class, fifty-percent of the students have no checkmarks. Zero. They have chosen, consciously or not, to be closest to people just like themselves. Now there are certainly many external factors that influence our pool of potential friendships. Despite the melting pot mythology of the United States, most of us live, work, and travel in relatively homogeneous circles. Our schools and communities are made up largely of people with similar socio-economic and racial backgrounds. By adding religion (and its weekly church services, bible studies, choral groups, and youth clubs) to the mix, you further limit the amount of interaction you're likely to have with people outside your own personal norm. The personal attribute of sexual orientation, which is still a polarizing issue in many parts of the country, circumscribes our choice of friends in several additional ways. If you're a member of a religious group that believes homosexuality is "against God's will" and will damn the sinner to eternal suffering in a fiery hell, you may never have known or spoken to an openly gay man or woman – or if you did, your mind was clenched shut. If you're of the opinion that homosexuality is fine if that's what "they" want but it's not something you want to be around, then you probably know gay men and women but choose to keep them at arm's length (or perhaps they choose to keep *you* at arm's length).

The point of this exercise is to think about how many opportunities for relationships we might have missed because of fear, distrust, contempt, or disapproval. To consider how our lives might have been improved and enriched by spending time to learn about different cultures, worldviews, and personal beliefs.

A lot of people have a bucket-list detailing all the things they want to do and places they want to go before they die. It's filled with things and places – not people. How much more robust and life-affirming would that bucket-list quest be if it included societal-focused activities like attending a service at every church, temple and mosque in your town – and talking one-to-one with the priest, rabbi, minister or imam? Hosting a potluck dinner with recent immigrants and demonstrating an appreciation for their culture and a profound respect for the courage it took to leave their homeland for a new life in a strange and scary place. That's a bucket list overflowing with meaning and import.

20/20 Sight Line: Explore Your Innate Biases

As stated on the Harvard University website, "Project Implicit is a non-profit organization and international collaboration between researchers who are interested in implicit social cognition – thoughts and feelings outside of conscious awareness and control. The goal of the organization is to educate the public about hidden biases and to provide a 'virtual laboratory' for collecting data on the Internet."

We have found the Implicit Association Test to be an eye-opening tool that will change the way you think about your attitudes and beliefs towards those who are different. Use this link to explore aspects of your core character that you never knew existed:

20-20MindSight.com/chapter3

CHAPTER 4: *"MOUNTAINTOPS AND VALLEYS"*

Embrace Your Weaknesses

I f you've never been less than perfect then you're not challenging yourself enough. That's the underlying philosophy of high achievers in every field from the arts and sciences to sports and business. These individuals embrace their weaknesses and readily acknowledge that they are not perfect. They don't pretend to know everything and they understand the inherent value of failure. "The *doer* makes mistakes," said the great basketball coach, John Wooden. "Mistakes come from doing, but so does success."

As a society we tend to celebrate success and vilify failure of any type. We're taught at an early age to strive for perfection – a straight-A report card, an Ivy League degree, and multiple job offers from Fortune 100 firms. The result is an often terrifying fear of failure. We don't want our mistakes to embarrass us or make us look foolish. That fear often puts the brakes on a wide variety of pursuits: everything from writing poetry, painting watercolors, asking out the cute Starbucks barista, starting a business, to requesting a promotion. We don't want to fail publicly, so we play it safe and only pursue those activities that offer a high probability of success. Arthur Miller, the great American playwright, explained why the safe path leads nowhere: "The best work that anybody ever writes is the work that is on the verge of embarrassing him, always."

If you doubt any of this, take a look back at some of the most admired minds throughout history. Galileo, Louis Pasteur, and Sigmund Freud were all ridiculed for their hypotheses and processes; but they all persevered and ultimately received their deserved acclaim. Most recently, the product that singlehandedly launched the mobile computing revolution, the iPhone, was almost universally lambasted by high-tech observers:

- "Apple is slated to come out with a new phone... And it will largely fail." *Michael Kanellos, CNET*
- "The iPhone is nothing more than a luxury bauble that will appeal to a few gadget freaks." *Matthew Lynn, Bloomberg*
- "There's no chance that the iPhone is going to get any significant market share. No chance." *Steve Ballmer, Microsoft CEO*

These comments seem laughable in retrospect, but what's even more absurd is that a similar torrent of ridicule greeted Apple's next breakthrough product, the iPad:

- "Behold The Apple iFlop: The iPad is a disappointing effort that fails to live up to the hype." *TheStreet.com*
- "The iPad is useless." *MSNBC*
- "Let's face it: the Apple iPad is a great big failure." *TechTalk*

The late Steve Jobs, the genius behind many of Apple's innovations, never cared what the critics thought of him or his company. All Jobs cared about was how Apple products would improve the lives of users. His flippant and often rude response to criticism was simply a manifestation of his laser focus on ignoring the fear of failure or embarrassment.

Steve Jobs was a marketer at his core, but he also embraced the fundamental tenet of scientific experimentation – i.e., success stems from an inevitable series of failures. Jobs was a legendary perfectionist, so it's safe to assume that early versions of the iPod, iPhone, etc. were abject failures to his critical eyes. Each iteration moved closer to Jobs' vision. Consumers, when presented with the final ready-for-prime-time product, couldn't even imagine the "failed" prototypes that had come before; and we bet the same was true for the Apple hardware and software engineers who designed the products.

"The best work that anybody ever writes is the work that is on the verge of embarrassing him, always."

Force Yourself To Fail

One way to help ensure that you achieve all you're capable of is to emulate the skill-building techniques of elite athletes – for whom success and failure are played out on a public stage for all to see. Wayne Gretzky would often push himself so hard in his solitary drills that he'd slip and tumble onto the ice. Tom Brady will throw into triple coverage in team practices because, as he explained in a *Boston Globe* interview, "You have to make the mistakes to learn from them. You never know how tight a window is until you throw it." Brady's coach, Bill Belichick agrees that practice is the time "to take risks... and to see how much you can do."

Mistakes define the route to success. In a sense, mistakes create brain connections that function in the same way as muscle memory. Many of the physical tasks we perform on a daily basis are done with little or no conscious effort. Examples of muscle memory include hitting a golf ball, touch-typing, and riding a bicycle; and they are all learned and ingrained by successful execution. Conversely, what we would call "behavioral memory" is learned from unsuccessful execution. So just as Tom Brady learns that forcing a pass will result in an interception, we will remember our failed attempt to ask for a raise, our clumsy expression of a contrary opinion that insults or angers the other party, and our workplace "shortcut" that ends up costing more in both time and money. And also like Brady, while we can't undo our mistake, we'll have the opportunity to modify our approach the next time out.

It sounds counterintuitive but striving for perfection and errorless execution leads to conformity and doing only what's expected. Taking a risk – while accepting the possibility of failure – is how breakthrough accomplishments are achieved and how genius rises above mediocrity. Winston Churchill eloquently applauded the character-building benefits of imperfection when he said, "Mountaintops inspire leaders but valleys mature them." The other key benefit in acknowledging your own imperfections and weaknesses is a greatly enhanced ability to accept the less-than stellar attributes of the people around us.

No one is perfect or should be expected to be perfect. If we can honor that truth in ourselves, we'll do the same with others.

*"Mountaintops inspire leaders but
valleys mature them."*

Perfection Is Not A Strength

Do you know the most commonly asked question at job interviews? It's this: *Name your greatest weakness.*

And the most common response to that question? *I'm a perfectionist.*

The question is bogus and the response is cloyingly worse. In defense of the interviewee, he or she is simply trying to turn a negative into a positive; but only the truly deluded could view perfectionism as a positive attribute. Perfection is illusory and its pursuit will inevitably lead to grief and disappointment. If you don't believe it, consider the arc of Tiger Woods' career. Woods was poised to reign as the greatest golfer of all time. His golf swing was a thing of beauty that combined power and finesse. But Woods was not content with an extraordinary swing. He wanted a perfect swing and he hired a succession of high-priced coaches to tweak and experiment with his mechanics. This ill-conceived pursuit of perfection resulted in a multi-year fall from the leaderboard to the middle of the pack. His extraordinary swing was a distant memory, and his perfect swing was a pipe dream.

We're quite certain we know what you're thinking: Even if perfection is unattainable doesn't it still serve a valid and useful purpose as an aspirational goal? The answer is an unequivocal no. The quest for perfection does not allow for mistakes or failure. Perfection cannot accommodate risk because risk entails too great a possibility of failure. A far better approach to achieving maximum performance in any endeavor we pursue is to embrace three simple tenets:

- *Focus on the journey not the destination.* Perfection implies an endpoint; but not only is that endpoint unattainable, it also mitigates the joy and self-satisfaction of achieving new milestones and new personal bests.

- *Strive for continual improvement rather than perfection.* All of the greatest hitters in Major League Baseball struck out far more times than they hit homeruns. Michael Jordan missed 50.3% of the shots he attempted (and 67.3% of three-point attempts), yet he is arguably the greatest NBA player of all time. Jordan certainly wanted to make every shot – and probably believed he could – but that was never his goal. He simply wanted to get better with every shot and every game. If perfection were his ultimate goal, he was an abject failure.

- *Learn with every step.* The key to embracing weakness is to learn from our mistakes and failures, and we do that by attending to our errors immediately – *as they occur.* Brain research has identified two types of behaviors when a mistake is made. The first is ignoring the mistake and moving on. The problem with this approach is the likelihood of repeating the mistake. That's why you'll see PGA golfers take another swing when an approach shot goes astray. They want to recognize and feel the difference between a good swing and a bad swing. The bad swing is in their immediate consciousness. If they waited until after the round, they wouldn't be able to compare the good and bad strokes. That approach by pro golfers exemplifies the second behavior type identified by researchers – focusing on the problem and determining how to correct it. Taken to its extreme, this idea of focusing on the problem can lead to "paralysis by analysis;" but as part of a well-rounded 20/20 mindset it will help you use weaknesses as a foundation for growth and success.

Admit It

One could make a strong argument that the three scariest words to state aloud (particularly in the workplace) are these: *I don't know.* That phrase is an explicit admission that we're less than perfect. Our fear of stating "I don't know" is amplified by the worries that we should know it, perhaps we once knew it but have since forgotten, and that everyone else knows it.

There are two alternative approaches to saying "I don't know." The first is to remain silent. You might look away and hide your head, try to change the subject, or excuse yourself to go to the bathroom or refill your coffee. The second, and far more damaging in the long run than admitting one's ignorance, is to act like you know. Think about times when you're asked a question and you're confident about the answer. Your response will be concise, definitive, and coherent. If you're anything like the rest of us, there have probably been occasions when you haven't known the answer to a question but felt compelled to respond nonetheless. In those situations your response was probably lengthy, convoluted, and effectively meaningless. We use far more words to cover up a lack of knowledge than when we actually know what we're talking about. And because we have no idea what the hell we're talking about, we're far more likely to commit a verbal faux pas that could haunt us in the future.

The moral of the story? Do not "fake it 'til you make it." Admit your ignorance and allow yourself to learn something in the process. Confessing that you are not an all-knowing automaton is a sign of self-confidence. It will demonstrate your integrity, engender respect and, most significantly, encourage others to embrace the same openness. The culture of an organization, community, or family can be positively impacted when people feel comfortable about sharing their shortcomings. Over time you'll experience a greater sense of teamwork, increased risk-taking, and more innovative thinking when the fear of looking dumb is removed. It's a win-win by any standard of measure.

20/20 Sight Line: Identify Your "Yes-Buts"

All of us have individual quirks and idiosyncrasies. There are some things we're good at and other things we're not so good at. The latter are the facets of our being that populate the "yes, but" statements that colleagues, friends, and family make (or silently think) about us. For example:

- "Yes, John is extremely talented, but he's late with every project."
- "Yes, Susan has great rapport with clients, but she treats her internal support team like indentured servants."
- "Yes, Eric is really great with numbers, but he refuses to help out with anything unless there's something in it for him."

29

Now identify three yes-buts of your own character

Yes, I, ———————————————— ,but I ————————————————— .

Yes, I, ———————————————— ,but I ————————————————— .

Yes, I, ———————————————— ,but I ————————————————— .

Rather than accepting your yes-buts as necessary evils, tackle them with commitment and urgency. Take each of these "but" statements and, in twenty-five words or less, write a game plan to address and correct them.

Turning a weakness into a strength is infinitely more satisfying that bulking up an existing strength. Turning a yes-but into a yes-and is nirvana.

Please visit us at **20-20MindSight.com/chapter4** to download the worksheet, access new content, see how others have completed the exercise, and maybe share your results.

CHAPTER 5: *"SINGING IN THE LIFEBOATS"*
Grit Your Teeth

The man whose name is synonymous with superhuman brainpower, Albert Einstein, attributed his myriad accomplishments not to the fact that "I'm so smart" but rather that "I stay with problems longer." Einstein's point is that intelligence, experience, and skill can only take you so far and do not constitute sure-fire pathways to success. Need proof? Just take a look back at your high school yearbook and see how many of the valedictorians, student council presidents, prom kings and queens, and most-likely-to-succeeds actually achieved their full potential. Then compare that to the number of under-the-radar, worker-bee students – the nerds, geeks, socially awkward, shy, quiet and the "uncool" masses – who exceeded everyone's wildest dreams. What matters most is not how much you know but how hard you work and how you put your knowledge and experience to work.

"Grit" is the buzzword du jour that explains Einstein's ability to "stay with problems longer." Moxie, resolve, and perseverance are equally apt descriptors. What all these words have in common is an infectious aggregation of discipline, passion, focus, and boundless enthusiasm – what we would call *irrepressibility*. Success in any long-term endeavor – whether the marathon of life or the foot-to-pavement reality of the Boston Marathon – requires filtering out distractions, rising above day-to-day adversities, and deferring reward and gratification. Rome may not have been built in a day, but our core values and character are rebuilt, solidified, and reinforced every single day of our lives. Unless, of course, we choose the easy way out and surrender at the first sign of adversity.

Life is hard. Work is hard. And success in life and work depends on a commitment to both the means and the end. Perseverance is easier when you have a clear goal in mind; and true success can only be achieved by putting in the requisite time and effort while eschewing shortcuts. The concert pianist Vladimir Horowitz adhered to a physically and mentally exhausting rehearsal schedule. He once said, "If I don't practice for a day, I know it. If I don't practice for two days, my wife knows it. If I don't practice for three days, the world knows it." Similarly elite athletes from Derek Jeter to Stephen Curry have always understood that if they slack off in practice they won't perform their best on game days. Irrepressibility is not a spigot you can turn on and off. It's a life force that guides and instructs how you spend every minute of every day.

One can debate the nature-or-nurture origins of irrepressibility, but its most salient characteristic – and by far the most critical component to reaping maximum benefit from this multi-faceted gift – is internalization. An irrepressible mindset is something to be purposefully and deeply embraced. Motivation, which is a core component of irrepressibility, comes in many forms – the exhortations of family and friends, the urgings of role models and mentors, and extrinsic rewards (i.e., fame and fortune). The common element among these motivational sources is externality. They reside outside your being, tend to be reactionary rather than proactive, and bring with them distinct disadvantages:

- They're usually transitory with little urgency or lasting power.
- They need continual reinforcement to be effective.
- They often lose their impact by over-use.
- They're made irrelevant by other environmental factors.

The truly irrepressible spirit resides within and is inextricably tied to one's core values and character. It's part of who you are and how you interact with the world. Martin Luther King Jr. perfectly captured the essence of internal motivation: "If you are called to be a street sweeper, sweep streets even as Michelangelo painted, or Beethoven composed music, or Shakespeare wrote poetry. Sweep streets so well that all the host of heaven and earth will pause to say, 'here lived a great street sweeper who did his job well.'"

Catch Yourself Doing Something Right

Ken Blanchard's classic book *The One-Minute Manager* urges managers to "catch someone doing something right" and then offer that person a face-to-face, one-minute praising. It's great advice and it works equally well with monitoring and nurturing one's own irrepressible mindset.

Because everyone is so busy these days, it's easy to gloss over milestones and ignore day-to-day accomplishments towards a long-term goal. But doing so represents missed opportunities to recognize real progress, reaffirm our commitments, appreciate the capabilities we too often take for granted, and refill our motivational fuel tanks.

In a perfect world this recognition for a job well done would be readily proffered by outside sources – bosses, colleagues, friends, and family. However, it's not a perfect world and never will be. Managers, coaches, and even loving family members and friends find it easier to criticize than praise. In the workplace, many managers purposely choose to withhold praise for their employees. Why? Because then they'll want more money or they'll get complacent and start slacking off. Plus they'll want more praise in the future, then other employees will expect to be praised otherwise they'll feel the manager is playing favorites, and it all takes too much time so let's just ignore it and remember to give'em a pat on the back at their annual performance review (if I even get around to doing one this year).

It's not just the workplace where praise is sparse. The Positive Coaching Alliance, whose mission is to "transform the culture of youth sports," hosts workshops for coaches to stress the importance of providing balanced feedback to their young athletes – both positive acknowledgment and constructive criticism. One of the exercises is to have the coaches toss out the kind of statements they would use to criticize players for a bonehead play. The put-downs – which tend to be specific, harshly personal, and borderline-cruel – come fast and furious and elicit loud hoots and guffaws. The scene changes dramatically when the PCA facilitator asks the coaches to share the positive statements they would offer players for well-executed plays. The affirmations are subdued and quite limited in number and scope – usually "Nice job" and "Atta boy" interspersed with the occasional "That's what I'm talking about."

We're not sure what it says about society that it's far easier for most people to criticize than praise, but it is a trait you can unlearn. And the best place to start is with yourself. Continue to search for ways to improve but also take the time to congratulate yourself for doing something right.

So What? Who Cares? And Other BFD Attributes Of Irrepressibility

Over the course of our careers and personal lives, we've had many people recount stories of mistakes they'd made and decisions that had gone terribly wrong. These stories are often accompanied by nervous stammering, tears, and/or physical trembling. We try to listen patiently and respond with understanding and empathy, after which we both tend to make the same simple observation that is almost universally applicable: "If that's the worst thing that ever happens to you, you'll live a long and happy life." The intent is to get the person to stop focusing on the past and start looking forward.

Just as coaches spend more time yelling at players than congratulating them, most people find it easier to immerse themselves in regret and self-flagellation rather than mindful self-discovery. One of Phil's favorite employees of all time once came into his office with a look so forlorn that Phil thought someone had died. The employee said he'd made a huge mistake and he was really sorry. He offered to write a check to cover the cost of the error. Phil asked him to sit down, take a deep breath, and explain what had happened. Turns out the company was hosting a sales conference and the employee had ordered a thousand pens imprinted with a custom logo. The problem was that he had given the vendor the wrong logo and all the pens were printed incorrectly. "They can't be used," he reported. Phil asked him if we could get a new batch in time for the meeting. He said yes. So Phil recapped the situation: the meeting attendees would get their pens with the correct logo and we were now the proud owners of one thousand additional pens sporting the wrong logo. "Which can't be used," he repeated. "Of course they can," Phil said. "They're fully functional. They do what pens do. Maybe they cost a bit more than the pens we normally buy, but they still get the job done, right?" That's when Phil uttered the "if this is the worst mistake you ever make..." comment. Phil knew when this young man left the office he took a life lesson with him; and today, as a senior manager at a major firm, he's passing along the same lesson to his staff.

There's a long list of adages that speak to this idea of viewing mishaps and disappointments from a different perspective. The most common is "when the world gives you lemons make lemonade." Our personal favorite is Voltaire's "Life is a shipwreck, but we must not forget to sing in the lifeboats." The most successful life journeys are guided with an attitude of "so what," "who cares," and "what difference does it really make?" This line of thought would likely strike many people as cavalier and scornful – and in the wrong hands it could indeed lead to callow indifference about the impact of one's actions. But as part of an irrepressible 20/20 mindset, it's an approach that can help reduce anxiety about immediate and seemingly urgent issues by viewing them in the context of the larger whole.

> ### "Life is a shipwreck, but we must not forget to sing in the lifeboats."

Irrepressible Doesn't Mean Irreversible

The very idea of quitting is anathema to most people (and Americans in particular). It's viewed as a sign of pitiful physical and mental weakness that goes against our can-do spirit of rugged individualism and national exceptionalism. Legendary football coach Vince Lombardi captured the essence of our disdain towards quitting in seven words: "Winners never quit and quitters never win." Like most aphorisms, Lombardi's statement has a simple structure and poetic cadence that lends it far more credibility than it deserves. That's right: *far more credibility than it deserves.*

Contrary to what you've been taught, quitting is not always a bad thing. In fact, quitting is often the best decision you can make. One of the things we can't control in this world is time, so it's clearly in our best interests to make the best use of the little time we have. Sometimes that means quitting. The trick is knowing when it makes sense to persevere and recognizing when it's time to quit.

If you're like most people, you grew up with ambitious, albeit unrealistic, career goals. Jillian's was to be a professional basketball player, pediatrician, author and politician...all at once. Phil's was to play centerfield for the New York Yankees. Others might have dreamt of becoming a best-selling novelist, an Oscar-winning actress, an undercover FBI agent, heart surgeon, or lead singer for a rock-and-roll band that's featured on the cover of the *Rolling Stone*. In Phil's case, he realized early on that the closest he'd ever get to centerfield in Yankee Stadium was a grandstand seat. If he hadn't abandoned that dream and instead stubbornly pursued it into his twenties and thirties, most people would have considered him deranged. They'd say he needed to get serious and get on with his life.

The same logic in support of quitting applies to pretty much every other aspect of our lives. Life is short so there is no reason to spend a single minute involved in a job, relationship, or activity that is not contributing to our sense of satisfaction and fulfillment. Investors are always advised not to throw good money after bad. The same is true of time. Why invest additional time in unsuitable, unhealthy, or downright harmful endeavors that have already gone on too long and show no signs of turning positive?

The decision to quit is among the hardest any of us ever makes. Why? Because we tend to look back instead of forward. We focus on the sunk costs – the time and energy we've already invested – and are hesitant to walk away and see all of it wasted. We often give more import to the time/money/energy we wasted than the time/money/energy we would waste by continuing on the same track.

Like you, we recognize that this advice seems to run counter to the whole spirit of grit and irrepressibility. In reality, however, the ability to quit, to say no, and to pursue new opportunities gets at the essence of the irrepressible 20/20 mindset. Irrepressibility is not mindlessness. It does not imply a naïve enthusiasm for every shiny object that captures your attention. Rather it provides a discerning perspective that helps us pick the spots where we can best fulfill our potential and contribute to the larger whole.

Run Like Secretariat

On June 9, 1973, Secretariat completed his sweep of horse racing's Triple Crown with a 31-length victory in the Belmont Stakes. Phil, whose father was a jockey's agent, literally gets shivers every time he watches a replay of that race. And when Phil watched the race play out in the film *Secretariat*, he literally cried.

As the race progressed, Secretariat and his arch-rival Sham were locked in a speed duel. The Belmont is a mile-and-a-half race – typically the longest distance any thoroughbred will ever run. Because of the distance, jockeys usually try to conserve the horse's energy in the early stages of the race.

Secretariat and Sham were running all out and not worried about conserving an ounce of anything. All the trackside prognosticators – including trainers, sportswriters, and other jockeys – were convinced that both horses would burn out and fade badly. That group included Secretariat's own handlers who shouted for Secretariat's jockey, Ron Turcotte, to slow down. Penny Tweedy, the experienced sportswoman who owned Secretariat, heard and understood the concerns – but she also knew Secretariat. Diane Lane, who gave a masterful performance as Tweedy, looked closely at Secretariat as he began to pull away from Sham. A look of maternal pride fills her face and she recognizes what's happening. She begins to shout, "Let him run, Ronnie. Let him run!"

What Tweedy realized was that Secretariat knew himself and his capabilities better than anyone else possibly could. And so she wanted the jockey to give the horse free rein to be himself and to accomplish all he was capable of. Mrs. Tweedy understood that Secretariat should not be constrained by conventional wisdom. He needed to be true to himself – and he needed someone to give him the opportunity to unleash his full potential. The rest is history.

So why did Phil cry during that scene? Because far too many people do not truly know themselves and appreciate the true extent of their abilities. They allow themselves to be held back by the desires and expectations of others. Secretariat could have won the Belmont by a single length and still be remembered as a Triple Crown champion. But if Turcotte had pulled back, the world would have been deprived of one of the greatest moments in sports history – and the true magic that resided within the greatest equine athlete in history.

So when it comes to irrepressibility, ask yourself if there's a jockey in your life with a tight hold on your reins? Have you achieved everything you're capable of? Ask yourself why and why not. Keep asking. And make sure you're the one controlling the reins to your own life.

20/20 Sight Line – The "Grit Scale"

In a November 2013 interview on NPR's "TED Radio Hour," Angela Duckworth defined grit as "the disposition to pursue very long-term goals with passion and perseverance." Duckworth is a Harvard- and Oxford-educated professor at the University of Pennsylvania who received a MacArthur Genius Grant for her work on the psychological origins and implications of grit. Professor Duckworth has studied West Point cadets, first-year teachers in tough inner city neighborhoods, and corporate salespeople to determine which individuals were most likely to stick it out through the hard times and achieve success in their given field. Through her research, Duckworth has identified grit as significantly more important in predicting success than traditional measures like IQ, emotional intelligence, and interpersonal skills.

One of Duckworth's findings is that grit can be learned and developed via practice and self-awareness. Professor Duckworth and UPenn offer several free online assessments of your grittiness. You can begin with the "12-Item Grit Scale" at: **20-20MindSight.com/chapter5**

As you work on ascending to the peak levels of irrepressible grit, keep in mind Winston Churchill's definition of true success and personal fulfillment: the "ability to go from failure to failure without losing your enthusiasm."

CHAPTER 6: "NOBODY SPEAKS THE TRUTH"

Never Disappoint

Whether you call it honesty, character, integrity, or trustworthiness, a well-defined personal honor code is arguably the most important component of the *20/20 Mind Sight* approach to life. Very few people would downplay the importance of honesty and integrity, yet we live in a world where we're surrounded by lies and distortions – both conscious and unconscious. Most of us have grown up with the concept of "white lies," but the line between victimless lies and irreparably damaging lies has been blurred and sometimes purposely erased.

The biggest lies of all are frequently the lies we tell ourselves – which then morph into the lies we tell and spread. Shakespeare's advice in *Hamlet* still rings true today:

> **"This above all, to thine own self be true;**
> **and it must follow as the night the day, thou**
> **canst not then be false to any man."**

Shakespeare wrote those words over four centuries ago, yet scant attention and little import are given to the *process* of learning how to be true to one's self. From pre-schools to the lecture halls of our great universities young people are tutored in facts and figures, they're tested and graded, and they are prodded and monitored within an inch of their lives. Rarely – if ever – are they encouraged to look inward and reflect on their character and core values. Ironically, this lack of introspection leads directly to the center-of-the-universe syndrome that in turn leads directly to the inability to recognize how our words and actions can negatively affect others.

A 20/20 mindset depends on a foundation of trust, and that bedrock is critical to building sincere, enduring, mutually beneficial relationships in the workplace, the community, within our own families, and with ourselves.

An Integral Component

The Irish novelist Elizabeth Bowen somewhat cynically observed, "Nobody speaks the truth when there is something they must have." Mark Twain made a similar observation about congressmen, suggesting that they would never lie "unless it was absolutely convenient." Bowen and Twain are both implying that people apply a situational definition to honesty and integrity. True character, however, imbued with immutable moral courage and steadfast values, allows for no compromise on honesty. Trustworthiness is not something one can compartmentalize and turn on or off at will. You can't be trustworthy in some aspects of your life but not in others. We are either trustworthy or we're not. We're either a rock or a pile of shifting sand. People either know they can count on us or we are doomed to disappoint them. It's an all or nothing proposition.

A basic tenet of Hinduism says, "If you speak the truth long enough, your word becomes universal law." Every time you demonstrate trust, you strengthen and enhance the public recognition of your integrity. That in turn leads to the ultimate goal of transforming the concept of trust into a practical and actionable reality. In a very real sense, trust becomes you and you become trust.

A Leap Of Faith

You cannot declare your trustworthiness. It's not something you can purchase, study up on, or "fake it until you make it." It must be genuine and it must be earned. Others must see your trustworthiness, recognize it, and declare it to themselves. That declaration of faith entails a substantial risk on the part of the "other" – a risk that many of us often ignore or don't even acknowledge. The risk that the other party is accepting involves a leap of faith that we will prove loyal and reliable. There is always the risk of failure in any endeavor, but trust engenders a safer environment where risks can be confidently calculated and failure is rare. That's exactly why untrustworthy acts create such angst among the wronged. Our trusting nature proved wrong. We were fooled and damaged in the process. And we'll be damned if we let it happen again.

The good news is that these leaps of faith work both ways. We take a leap every time we trust others, and they take a leap when they place trust in us. That means each of us can play a significant role in increasing trustworthiness across society. If you want to be trusted, set a standard of honesty and integrity for others to follow. Think about what you expect from others and demand the same from yourself. And repeat. Aristotle offered crisp and timeless advice on this topic in his *On Education*. Aristotle believed that we learn the virtues of character by acting out those virtues – via imitation, practice and repetition: "*We become just by doing just acts, temperate by doing temperate acts, brave by doing brave acts.*" In this much-quoted statement, Aristotle describes a virtuous circle of integrity. As we model trustworthiness by doing trustworthy acts, we become more trustworthy. More importantly, as we manifest trust in our day-to-day dealings we serve as a model for others to emulate. We engender trust by modeling trust – which will in turn engender trustworthiness in others. And so on.

One of Us Is Lying

Several years ago a former colleague of Phil's – let's call her Kristen – was engaged in a compensation dispute with her boss, who happened to be the CEO of the company. It was a classic he-said/she-said situation. Here's the scenario in brief. The company was rolling out a new compensation program and when the CEO explained the specifics of her target amount, Kristen said it was insufficient and substantially lower than her peers. She suggested that she and the company part amicably rather than engaging in a pissing contest. The CEO quickly agreed that Kristen's package was lower than her colleagues and assured her that the discrepancy would be adjusted by a certain date. Just as they had done on previous occasions, they shook hands on the deal.

When the agreed-upon date arrived, the extra compensation did not arrive along with it. The CEO acknowledged his earlier assurances but stated it was now out of his hands. Kristen was justifiably upset. The additional compensation was being paid out to her colleagues and she was low girl on the totem pole. She offered to resign and not make a fuss as long as she was paid the amount she was due. The CEO warned that she was going down a slippery slope and said the discussion was over.

Kristen subsequently sued the company and endured a bitter legal battle that was ultimately settled out of court. The company's other employees were forced to take a position – either side with the CEO and ostracize their colleague, or side with Kristen. All of this position-taking, however, was done with no one knowing all the facts of the matter. And because it was a legal matter, Kristen was unable to share any non-public information. Instead, she made the same statement to anyone who inquired: "Only two people know the truth. One of us is lying. You decide who."

That statement usually engendered a smirk and a knowing nod. Kristen had spent her entire career building a reputation for integrity, frankness, and honest dealing. She felt confident that the vast majority of people would look at the two parties and be hard-pressed to identify any instance where Kristen had ever said or done anything that could remotely be construed as untoward or deceitful.

We share this story to ask if you would be confident in declaring that "One of us is lying" and leaving the determination to others. If you can, then give yourself a hearty pat on the back. If you can't, start today building a reputation as a person of honesty and principle. Doing so will enrich your life in multiple ways and will do the same for your family, friends, and colleagues.

The Honest Apology

Even the most honest and dependable of us will occasionally make mistakes and do or say something we wish we could take back. Those moments often cause feelings of fear and humiliation and constitute a critical inflection point where the rubber of trustworthiness hits the road in earnest. That inflection point relates to a longstanding debate in the business world regarding the difference between responsibility and accountability. In simplest terms responsibility is given to someone (usually because of function or title) while accountability must be taken, owned, and embraced by the individual. Responsibility is general in scope while accountability is specific and personal. Very personal. When things go wrong in the workplace some "responsible" employees will point the finger of accountability, and the accompanying blame, at others (usually subordinates or weaker peers). These individuals covet the prestige and reward of responsibility (usually in the form of money and promotions) but want no exposure to the downside of personal accountability. These individuals roam aimlessly down a self-indulgent path of inured idiocy and add nothing to our discussion of personal integrity.

Our focus instead is on those individuals who unflinchingly and without hesitation hold themselves accountable. They've already decided to own up to their failings and foibles, but that's not their only decision. They must now make a deliberate choice between offering an apology or a confession. Notwithstanding the more common connotations of confession related to criminal activities and religious traditions, heartfelt confessions play an important role in 20/20 value systems.

In *The Art of the Public Grovel*, Susan Wise Bauer offers a distinction between apologies and confessions: "An apology is an expression of regret. *I am sorry*. A confession is an admission of fault. *I am sorry because I did wrong*." As much as we like the simplicity of Bauer's definition, it's a little too simplistic. We've all seen a parade of politicians standing alongside their stoic wives as they "confessed" their affairs, multiple encounters with prostitutes, and addiction to sexting with underage interns. Holding back tears, they admit that they "did wrong" and invariably ask the Lord's help in becoming a better person. But it all comes across as hollow and banal.

Individuals possessing a 20/20 mindset make a more nuanced distinction between apologies and confessions (even if they don't use that exact terminology). Apologies are usually offered in less public, less official, and less specific ways than the offense that preceded them. Confessions include a true profession of accountability (without the subtle and not-so-subtle caveats that accompany most apologies). The key difference is that confessions include an articulated action plan to make amends and to ensure the mistake/offense is not repeated. Confessions also include a deep understanding that our internal compass has misfired and needs to be recalibrated to recognize dangers and obstacles long before we collide head-on into them.

This type of confession is sometimes referred to as moral courage – a solidarity of mind and spirit that can stare down any challenge and, in the process, allow you to scale ever greater heights.

20/20 Sight Line: "Integrity and Work Ethics Test"
Our favorite definition of integrity comes from the Irish author C.S. Lewis: "Doing the right thing, even when no one is watching." And therein lies the conundrum. If no one is watching, then how can integrity truly be measured and monitored? The honest answer is "with great difficulty." Nonetheless, because we believe integrity represents the foundation of a life well lived, we searched for a tool that would provide some insight into one's personal approach to integrity, honesty, and ethics. You can access that online survey at: **20-20MindSight.com/chapter6**

Put Intelligence In Its Place

Here's the irony of ironies: Alfred Binet, one of the creators of the modern IQ test, developed the test at the request of the French government to identify children who had learning disabilities and needed special educational services. Shortly thereafter many educators and psychologists began promoting Binet's creation as a means of measuring and comparing intelligence levels. Binet was dismayed by this co-optation and was quite vocal about the test's limitations. He argued that there were innumerable aspects of intelligence that could not be squeezed onto a linear scale. In addition, Binet was concerned that IQ scores would be construed as a fixed marker of an individual's intellectual capabilities – i.e., once intelligent, always intelligent. Binet believed strongly that intelligence should not be viewed as an end onto itself. Rather, intelligence was one of many variables of the human journey and would fluctuate in the same way as our physical abilities.

Despite the protests of Binet and countless others, intelligence is still widely viewed as being highly correlated to standardized test scores and academic degrees. The counterpoint, however, is the empirical evidence that "highly intelligent" people – i.e., those with high scores on SATs and GREs, multiple degrees from prestigious universities, and impressive-sounding job titles – can be boorishly unaware, unrealistic, and uninformed. At the extremes, many so-called intelligent people can be downright dumb and remarkably ineffective. Part of this divergence can certainly be attributed to Emotional Intelligence, the concept introduced by Daniel Goleman that focuses on how well people perceive, use, understand, and manage emotions in themselves and others. An equally important factor is the breadth of one's experience and perspective – how *informed* they are about the world and people beyond the confines of their own skin and day-to-day lives.

Think about it from this perspective. Just as there's a huge difference between being ignorant and ill-informed, there's an equally vast difference between being intelligent and being well-informed. Intelligence, charm, and cleverness are overrated while the acts of observing, interpreting, and synthesizing are underappreciated. Earl Weaver, the Hall of Fame manager of the Baltimore Orioles expressed it this way:

"What counts is what you learn after you know it all."

See The Light

The genius of the truly intelligent is that the more they know, the more they know there is to know. That's why there are so few actual geniuses in the world. Run-of-the-mill intelligentsia often clutch their knowledge so tightly that they will resist change even when faced with new information. That's when knowledge and fact turn into intransigent belief and faith – i.e., "it's true because I believe it's true" (or want it to be true).

Intransigent intelligence results from fear and indoctrination. It is far removed from mature wisdom and understanding – both of which require continual questioning and probing. True intelligence is achieved with wide-open eyes, ears, heart, and mind. Intransigent intelligence is arrogant and condescending and arises from purposeful blindness. To put it as simply as possible, intransigent intelligence is stupidity in the fullest sense of the word.

To be fair, some of this intransigence – especially among those with an expertise in a given discipline – is due to the widespread but misunderstood Curse of Knowledge. The more people know about a particular topic the less capable they tend to be in sharing that information simply and effectively. They have a hard time getting out of their own heads. They provide far too much detail and get too deep into the minutiae of the topic before painting a broad-brush picture. You want to know the time and they tell you how to build a watch. In some cases experts only know what they know and, even worse, think that's all there is to know.

In many ways this focus on being *informed* rather than *intelligent* provides another perspective on mindfulness. The informed mindset takes in all the data and stimuli in its path – not just the particulars it agrees with. Informed individuals want to be challenged. They perceive problems differently and, as a direct result, create solutions that evade others. Most simply the informed 20/20 mindset casts a broad light on all it encounters. The Hindus refer to this light as *consciousness* and believe, "One who kindles the light of awareness within gets true light."

> **"Informed individuals want to be challenged.**
> **They perceive problems differently and, as a direct**
> **result, create solutions that evade others."**

Get Real

Most people are ridiculously over-confident about their abilities. In survey after survey they consistently rate themselves as above average on positive traits (e.g., empathy and creativity) and below average on negative traits (e.g., dishonesty and pushiness). In a study conducted by Allstate Insurance, a full 93% of respondents considered themselves to be above-average drivers. This inability to accurately judge one's competence and capabilities is actually quite diabolical. In scientific circles The Dunning-Kruger effect describes the cognitive bias wherein incompetent individuals substantially overestimate their abilities, while those with demonstrable skills underestimate their competence compared with others. The Downing effect similarly describes the pervasiveness of illusory superiority with a focus on the tendency of highly intelligent people to underestimate their intelligence, while their low-intelligence counterparts exaggerate theirs.

The harshest manifestation of this inability to recognize and internalize one's abilities and accomplishments is the Impostor Syndrome. It's a surprisingly common disorder that afflicts young and old, male and female, hourly workers and C-level executives. (Note: The Impostor Syndrome concept was introduced in 1978 as part of a psychological study of successful women who couldn't accept their successes. While it's difficult to prove that women are more prone to questioning their ability, it has been demonstrated that women are more likely to publicly admit to facing this challenge.)

The Imposter Syndrome revolves around a self-fulfilling prophecy of failure that stops people from achieving their full potential and enjoying the pleasure of a job well done. Consider these statements from rich, famous, and beautiful award-winning actresses:

- Emma Watson: "Any moment, someone's going to find out I'm a total fraud. I can't possibly live up to what everyone thinks I am."
- Michelle Pfeiffer: "I still think people will find out that I'm really not very talented. I'm really not very good. It's all been a big sham."
- Meryl Streep: "Why would anyone want to see me again in a movie? ...I don't know how to act anyway, so why am I doing this?"

Let's now add another name to that list: Jillian in her own words.

As a teenager, basketball was the centerpiece of my life. It was the one thing I loved. It helped me escape and allowed me to engage my body and mind at the same time. I loved how basketball challenged me. I taught myself to dribble and shoot with both hands. I studied the statistics of other teams and players so I could devise a game plan accordingly. I practiced daily including most nights outside on the dirt driveway under the flickering spotlight that my Dad had draped across the treetops. I put in countless hours of practice and it paid off. As a thirteen-year-old I was invited to skip from the junior high school team to the varsity team.

That's when I started to freeze. It was not a case of the nerves in the way that most people would describe it. Instead I was overwhelmed with the gut-wrenching fear that everyone would eventually figure out that I wasn't as good as they thought. That I was in fact nothing but a fraud, just the beneficiary of someone's error in judgment.

My response was to shut down, quite literally. No one could understand it and many people became very upset with me. I, of course, interpreted this as validation that I really wasn't as good as they thought. I remember shooting around before practices and games either by myself or with one trusted teammate. I could drain shot after shot lefty or righty from anywhere on the court. Once the rest of the team and coaches showed up, however, I would not take a single shot. I was petrified that I wouldn't measure up. That I'd be rejected for not being good enough.

Fast-forward about 15 years and I found myself at a coffee meeting with an internationally successful businessman. As we talked about our backgrounds and experiences, I learned that it was rare for him to have get-to-know-you meetings – especially with folks of my lowly rank and stature in the business world. His schedule was such that he had to be highly protective of his time. At the moment I didn't understand why he would tell me this or, more to the point, why he would make an exception for little old me.

As we sipped our coffee and talked about our respective passions, fears, and aspirations we established a strong bond and both of us felt like we had been friends for years. It was that deep connection that prompted him to share an observation that changed my life: "You're like the poster child for the Impostor Syndrome." He said it in a way that clearly implied I already knew that about myself. In reality I'd never heard the term before; but as he formed the words, a rush of warm relief ricocheted through my body. For the first time in my life I had a framework to understand why I continually got caught in a mental vortex of doubt. In addition to understanding why I often struggled, it was an invaluable revelation to learn that I was not alone and that many others faced similar hesitations and fears.

Jillian still experiences the pangs of the Impostor Syndrome; but she's been able to recognize the symptoms and her remedy is to focus on the task at hand, do the best she can, and refrain from second-guessing and prejudgment. She's also been able to embrace and accept her skill set by observing the positive way people react to her and acknowledging the value she delivers to her clients.

Know When To Run

A few years ago Jillian received a call from a colleague inviting her to a meet-and-greet with some high-level state politicians. The woman had been asked to access her network and introduce people who would make effective political candidates. Jillian's was one of the first names that came to mind. At the event, Jillian focused on listening intently. She deliberately suspended her own thoughts and judgments about the various topics being discussed. Most importantly, she was monitoring her feelings as she listened. Some of what Jillian learned that night intrigued her to the point that she agreed to meet with a prospective campaign manager. When he asked if Jillian could see herself as an elected State Representative, she told him, "Absolutely. If I do choose to run for office, I will win. Period."

As the conversation progressed and Jillian attended additional meetings with other state politicians and operatives, she realized they were making assumptions, jumping to conclusions, and seeing her through a self-serving lens. This caused an epiphany of sorts, and Jillian took a step back and asked herself, *if all these people describe me as such, is that in fact who I am?* The answer was obvious. She was not who they needed her to be – nor did she want to become that person. She began to feel totally disconnected from these people. Their polarized perspective reminded her of a grade-school playground. Jillian would be on the "yellow" team and the party line was that they were way better than the "green" team. It struck her as an "Us vs. Them" pep rally, and she wanted no part of it.

Jillian's decision not to run for office highlights our deeply held belief that it's okay to walk away from opportunities that aren't right for you. Indeed sometimes quitting – or refusing to start in the first place – is the only thing to do. Every opportunity you choose to pursue represents another opportunity you won't have the time or resources to pursue. Every decision represents a trade-off. More of this means less of that. It's a delicate balancing act between ambition and genuine purpose. The best way to maintain that balance is to listen to the unfiltered information your heart and mind are feeding you. How do you feel about the trade-offs? Are you being motivated by the desire to contribute to the greater good or is it merely a personal ego trip? Does the opportunity bring you one step closer to your long-term aspirations and personal goals?

Had Jillian chosen run for office – regardless of whether she won or lost – the campaign would have permanently morphed her personal brand and compromised the person she'd worked so hard to become. She chose wisely and we recommend you do the same. Just because you can do something doesn't mean you should.

> ### *"Just because you can do something doesn't mean you should."*

Look Ahead

The "post-mortem" is a well-established organizational technique to review the good and bad of a completed project. It's akin to a medical autopsy to determine the cause of death; but just like an autopsy, it does nothing to benefit the now-deceased patient or the completed, albeit flawed, project. The post-mortem is designed to identify problems so as to not repeat them; nonetheless lessons taught via post-mortems are rarely lessons learned and future projects continue to fail. Why? Because we seem to be hardwired to charge ahead and get working before we have a viable and thoroughly scrutinized plan. "Time's a wastin" is the all-too-frequent battle cry in our personal and professional lives.

Albert Einstein advocated a markedly different approach: "If I had an hour to solve a problem, I would spend 55 minutes thinking about the problem and five minutes thinking about solutions." Einstein valued the pre-mortem more than the post-mortem. He knew that an effective solution could only arise from an in-depth analysis of the problem – *before* getting to work on solving it.

The pre-mortem consists of poking and probing. In the business world begin by asking why and why not. Determining whether the problem needs to be addressed at all. Deciding whether to pursue a fix or a replacement. Thoroughly considering the ramifications of every possible approach.

If it's an interpersonal problem, put yourself in the other person's shoes. Consider what they're feeling, what they're afraid of, and what solution they're hoping for. Control your own emotional feelings and decide what you want to accomplish and envision how you see the relationship continuing in the future.

It all comes down to preparation, foresight and insight. The 20/20 mindset has no preconceived notions or solutions. Instead it can see both the forest and the trees. It recognizes both opportunities and black holes for what they are. It won't be able to avoid every black hole but it will be ready to seize genuine opportunities whenever they arise.

20/20 Sight Line: Emotional Intelligence

We mentioned Daniel Goleman's concept of emotional intelligence only in passing earlier in this chapter because several best-selling books and dozens of articles have been written about it. We view emotional intelligence as the intersection of emotions and thoughts and, as such, consider it critically important to building a 20/20 mindset.

Similar to measuring honesty, however, it's difficult to gauge one's EQ solely on the basis of a questionnaire. There are some consultants and personal coaches who will conduct in-depth EQ analyses, but they are very expensive and beyond the means of most individuals. We have, however, discovered an online survey that you can access at:

20-20MindSight.com/chapter7

CHAPTER 8: *"A KIND OF SALVATION"*

Face Down Your Fears

One of Phil's students was the punter on a Division 1 football team. He explained that he had once experienced an epiphany regarding the value of the inner peace and confidence derived from self-reflection. It occurred he said, "When I accepted what would happen if I dropped a ball in front of 80,000 people along with ESPN's national TV cameras. I almost had to become okay with the outcome before I was able to have it not happen to me." What he realized was that even a mistake on as grand a stage as a primetime ESPN telecast would have no meaningful impact on his life or character. His family and friends would still love him. He would still possess all his intellectual and physical skills. He would indeed be sorry for having made the mistake; but he understood it had nothing to do with how hard he was playing, how importantly he valued his team's success, or how he would remember his football career when his playing days were over. It would be a blip – and a blip is nothing to be feared.

Fear is an affect. It's a powerful emotion that bubbles up from deep inside. When you combine that understanding with the fact that the word *courage* derives from the Latin word for *heart*, it's an easy extrapolation to the concept that most of the fears that hold us back are internal rather than external. Fear is based on feelings not logic. It is a hard-wired response to every threat – real or imagined. But even if the threat is only imagined, it doesn't make the fear any less real or painful. Unless addressed, fear can be a constant tormentor. Our deepest fears do not come and go. They are always present in the back of the mind – at least until a catalyst propels them front and center. Or, as with our introspective punter, until a 20/20 epiphany repels our fears and relegates them to the trash heap of our psyche.

> **"Most of the fears that hold us back are internal rather than external. Fear is based on feelings not logic."**

Freedom From Fear

Every school child can recite the exhortation from President Franklin Roosevelt's first inaugural address that "the only thing we have to fear is fear itself." Fewer of us remember FDR's revisiting of this theme in his State of the Union address to Congress in 1941:

> *In the future days, which we seek to make secure, we look forward to a world founded upon four essential human freedoms. The first is freedom of speech and expression...The second is freedom of every person to worship God in his own way...The third is freedom from want...* ***The fourth is freedom from fear.***

Roosevelt understood that fear is an insidious form of oppression. It holds us back and severely limits what we can aspire to or accomplish. Indeed, Roosevelt further defined fear as a "nameless, unreasoning, unjustified terror which paralyzes." Our Founding Fathers incorporated a similar sentiment in the Declaration of Independence when they identified "the pursuit of happiness" as an unalienable right. No one can truly be happy if he's afraid. Fear is debilitating, and it's all for naught. Fear saps our strength and wastes both time and energy. It's like the concept of "wasted calories" in reverse. We expend a great amount of energy without reaping any benefit.

"Fear is an insidious form of oppression."

In a very real sense, fear is a choice. Abraham Maslow, the American psychologist who is best known for his "hierarchy of needs," believed that every single day, in most everything we do, we have the choice to move forward and grow or step backward into our safety net. In his classic *Toward a Psychology of Being*, Maslow explains:

> *Every human has both sets of forces within him. One set clings to safety and defensiveness out of fear, tending to regress backward, hanging on to the past...afraid to take chances, afraid to jeopardize what he already has, afraid of independence, freedom and separateness. The other set of forces impels him forward toward wholeness of Self and uniqueness of Self, toward full functioning of all his capacities, toward confidence in the face of the external world.*

Maslow created this schema to illustrate the human dilemma and provide a solution to our internal conflict:

Enhance the dangers   Enhance the attractions

SAFETY ◄◄ **PERSON** ►► GROWTH

Minimize the dangers   Minimize the attractions

The idea is to strengthen the growth-oriented mechanisms and thought processes (by making them more attractive and less dangerous) while weakening the safety-oriented concerns (by making them less attractive and more problematic). The paths of growth and safety possess both "anxieties and delights." In Maslow's words, "We grow forward when the delights of growth and anxieties of safety are greater than the anxieties of growth and the delights of safety."

Enhance the dangers	Enhance the attractions
• It's perfectly natural to be nervous. • If you choose not to speak, probably won't be asked again. • Will regret passing on the opportunity. • Will envy the person who speaks in your place.	• High visibility opportunity. • An honor to be asked to speak. • Audience will perceive you as a leader. • Audience will envy you. • Audience wants you to do well.

SAFETY ◀◀ PERSON ▶▶ GROWTH

• Presentation will be over before you know it. • Your presentation doesn't have to be perfect to be successful.	• Presentation will be over before you know it. • You know the content and will be delivering information of value.
Minimize the dangers	**Minimize the attractions**

The growth and safety issues that Maslow discusses – and their resultant fears – are not necessarily of huge import or consequence. They often represent commonplace aspects of our day-to-day lives – e.g., applying for a new job, requesting a promotion or raise, introducing ourselves to the cute waitress we see at our favorite diner, writing a letter to the editor of the local newspaper, advocating on behalf of another, expressing love, offering constructive feedback to a friend or colleague, or giving a presentation. That last example, public speaking, is frequently cited as the number one fear of the average American – so let's use that fear to illustrate Maslow's theory about the inner conflict between growth and safety. To someone who truly fears giving presentations, the initial response to a speaking opportunity is to consider all the things that could go wrong: you'll trip moving onto the stage; you'll freeze and be unable to speak; you'll mumble; you'll speak way too fast; you'll lose your place; you'll ignore the audience; and people will laugh in all the wrong places. Most people with a fear of public speaking (or any fear, for that matter) usually ignore all the good things that could accrue as a result of the opportunity. Because of that propensity, it's a good idea to begin your analysis on the "growth" side of the equation. First off, go back and review all the things that could possibly go wrong. You'll see that they share a common element – a fixation on how the audience will react to you. The key then is to borrow from Aikido, a Japanese martial art that uses the opponent's strength and power against him. In the context of public speaking, you want to convert your fear of the audience into a positive. Yes, the audience will be watching you; but they're happy for you, are interested in what you have to say, and want you to succeed. In addition, because you know the content as well or better than anyone, you'll be delivering information of value. Even if you believe that you are "not worthy," you can believe that your content is.

Moving to the safety side of Maslow's schema, you start by reminding yourself that the event will be done and behind you in a nanosecond. You've probably already spent more time and energy worrying about the presentation than you'll expend delivering it. Consider that when the big day arrives and you're watching someone else speak in your place, you're going to regret the decision to waste a precious opportunity to move your career ahead. And perhaps most importantly, remind yourself that you're not alone. It's natural to be nervous. It's also natural to make mistakes and occasionally stumble with your words. It's happened to every great orator from Lincoln to Churchill to Obama. Just think about the presenters at the Academy Awards live television program. These are people who make a living in front of audiences and cameras. They're reading from cue cards; and they still mess up. Why should you be perfect when they're not? And why would you expect yourself to be?

Doesn't it sound so simple and rational? As rational creatures, we should be able to use this same kind of schematic approach to address all of our fears. Unfortunately many, if not most, of our fears are decidedly irrational. They are based on internal emotions and conflicts between the heart and psyche. Eliminating them requires more than a comparison of pros and cons. It requires a whole different mindset.

Fear Of Freedom
FDR and others have spoken eloquently about "freedom from fear," but few have addressed the deeply felt, albeit rarely acknowledged, fear of freedom. As counterintuitive as it may sound, there is indeed a pervasive

fear of freedom around the world. The German philosopher and psychologist Erich Fromm believed it was an innate characteristic of our species. In *Escape From Freedom*, Fromm described the human tendency to "give up the independence of one's own individual self and to fuse one's self with somebody or something outside of oneself in order to acquire the strength which the individual self is lacking." The American educator, John Dewey, took a similar stance:

> **"It is the existence within our own personal attitudes and within our own institutions of conditions which have given a victory to external authority, discipline, uniformity and dependence."**

We would take the concept even further. One of the catalysts for this book was a study conducted by John Collard of Yale's Institute of Human Relations. Dr. Collard described seven common fears. Six of them are of the run-of-the-mill variety, but one jumped out: the fear of thinking. It was a concise distillation of the lessons we most often emphasized with our clients and students. The key to personal and professional success is the ability to think for oneself. It's a commonsense truism yet it's rarely adhered to or embraced. It's not an overstatement to say that many of us have relinquished our minds to our parents, churches, employers, governments, and political parties. For a country that prides itself on its rugged individualist roots, the U.S. is increasingly a nation of compromisers and weak-kneed sycophants. A nation of non-thinkers that communicates primarily via sound bites, half-truths, and outright deception. The rote, repetitive regurgitation that we discuss elsewhere in the book has become the modern-day substitute for critical thinking. If we see or hear something from a talking head on television, from the pulpit, from a web newsfeed, or on Twitter, YouTube, Facebook, Tumblr, or whatever happens to be the next great social-media site, we grant it instant credibility. We pass it on, it goes viral, and it becomes gospel.

In a sense, we've become conduits for the beliefs of others. It's so much easier and safer to leave the hard work of thinking to a third party. The alternative would be to create our own thoughts and opinions, and that is a terrifying prospect for many people. It forces us to take a stand against "them" – the people, organizations, and ideologies we have empowered to control our hearts and minds. Maslow wrote of the intense loneliness that accompanies any act of creative thinking that dares to threaten the status quo. He said, "It is precisely the god-like in ourselves that we are ambivalent about, fascinated by and fearful of, motivated to and defensive against." The reason, Maslow explained, is that the discovery of a great talent in oneself "can certainly bring exhilaration but it also brings a fear of the dangers and responsibilities and duties of being a leader and of being all alone."

The key to personal and professional success is the ability to think for oneself.

Our greatest strength as humans is our ability to reason. It is also our most delimiting weakness. We humans possess a profound sense of self-consciousness and are keenly aware of our individual uniqueness. We recognize ourselves as separate and distinct entities; yet we also understand the immensity of the universe and our place as the tiniest of specks in both the natural and supernatural worlds. It is no wonder then that we often see ourselves as unworthy and insignificant. It is that perception of our insignificance that constrains our ability and desire to give our self-identity full expression.

It is an ironic dichotomy. We see ourselves as unique beings floating among billions of equally unique beings. Our uniqueness makes us incredibly powerful, yet the one-in-many-billions aspect of the world makes us feel meaningless and irrelevant. That realization contributes to the pervasive belief that our lives don't matter and, even worse, our thoughts, beliefs, and feelings don't matter. That's a terrifying concept and the remedy is to tightly link our thoughts, beliefs, and feelings to others. Doing so transfers responsibility for our words and actions to the other party and provides cover for our beliefs. We leave the thinking to others so we don't have to think for ourselves.

The fears that arise from this abdication of thinking are not the commonly recognized phobias related to the aforementioned public speaking or the widespread fear of snakes, spiders, or heights. Instead, they are the fears that result directly from a lack of self-reflection and self-knowledge. These are the fears that a 20/20 mindset can turn into acts of courage.

Specifically: the courage to be alone, to make mistakes, to trust and be trusted, to commit, to question, to respond, to accept and reject, to age and, most importantly, to ask what would I do if I wasn't afraid? In many cases, the things you would do if you weren't afraid are indeed the very things you should be doing to live a life of fulfillment.

If you only had the courage to live such a life.

Fear And Courage

Courage is not the opposite of fear, nor does it imply a lack of fear. The two are inextricably linked. And just as fear is a choice, so is courage. General Omar Bradley, who had over one million troops under his command in World War II, defined courage as "the capacity to perform properly even when scared half to death." Courage is the ability to do what we need to do in the face of our fear. Courage in the face of fear is what enables such disparate activities as firemen rushing into a burning building, corporate whistleblowers reporting the illegal or unethical actions of their employers, and young homosexuals coming out to their disapproving parents.

Referring back to Maslow's safety/growth schema, we have the fear *of* something while simultaneously having the courage *to do* something. The "enhanced attractiveness" of doing something includes the euphoria that results from facing down a fear. Our initial fright transforms itself into feelings of excitement, extreme focus and, ultimately, pride. Jillian often points to her experiences when skydiving and surfing for the first time. She used those physical activities as a means to explore how her mind and body handled fear and then turned her success into a personal epiphany. She realized the truth in Plato's observation that "Courage is a kind of salvation" – a salvation that will live within us forever.

The good news is that we have multiple opportunities every day to let our courage shine brightly and powerfully. When you pare it down to its essence, most every act of courage can be categorized in one of these five groupings:

The Courage To Try – The most prevalent fears we face on a daily basis are the fear of failure and the fear of rejection. The safety-focused response is to not even try, to give up before you've started. The foundation for these fears is low self-esteem and a lack of confidence. We decide that the risk-reward calculation is out of balance. The odds of being rewarded are remote at best. We convince ourselves that we'd never get the promotion so why even apply for it. Similarly, there's no way the cute neighbor who just moved in would ever consider going out with us so why bother starting a conversation. The 20/20 approach to boosting your courage and giving something a try is to consider the worst-case scenario. You don't get the promotion and you don't get the date. So what? Nothing has changed in your life. In fact, from a holistic perspective, you've added another life experience to learn from. And from that same holistic perspective, it is far better to regret the things you did or attempted, rather than the things you were afraid to do.

The Courage To Question – Blind faith refers to beliefs that are held without true understanding, reasoned discrimination, or experiential proof. While an argument can be made that all faith is blind by definition, for our purposes we'll focus on the articles of faith that can derail interpersonal relationships and our life's journey towards self-knowledge, fulfillment, and community. Take a moment to consider your most deeply held beliefs and then focus on those that originated from an external source. The beliefs you hold because you were taught to hold them. Examples might include the belief that women are subservient (and belong in the kitchen and out of the boardroom), homosexuality is an abomination (and gay marriage will destroy traditional marriage), Muslims are terrorists (and shouldn't be allowed to build mosques in "our" neighborhood), Jews are stingy and greedy (and plotting to take over the world), and Mexicans are lazy (and so we have to build an electrified fence on our southern border to keep them out and stop them from taking our jobs). No one – and we truly mean no one – ever derived these beliefs on his or her own. They are the result of indoctrination by one or more of the groups we belong to and the lack of a questioning mindset of our own. One need look no further for proof than the racial divide between whites and blacks in the United States. Many Ku Klux Klan members – as well as millions of unabashed bigots – counted individual blacks among their friends, yet hated blacks as a group. That seems like an irreconcilable conflict yet is a surprisingly common mindset. The remedy to this kind of built-in bias is to ask yourself probing questions that you answer honestly and thoughtfully. For example:

- Will my relationship with the opposite sex truly be threatened by gay marriage? How and why?
- Is our treatment of Muslim Americans after the attacks in Paris and San Bernardino similar to the shameful treatment of Japanese Americans following Pearl Harbor? Why don't we similarly lump together and hate all Catholics for the actions of pedophile priests? And while we're targeting large swaths of Americans how about the young white men who committed the atrocities in Charleston, Aurora, and Sandy Hook?
- Why do women need to endure invasive and demeaning procedures in order to exercise their legal right to an abortion? Who benefits from these requirements? How and why?

We've long been advocates of playing the role of the devil's advocate in business, but the approach works equally well in our personal lives. The vast majority of our beliefs could be strengthened – or decimated – simply by tossing a monkey wrench into the mix. Unfortunately, it's a technique that requires a level of confidence and spiritual courage that is rarely found in a society that celebrates consensus and frowns upon intellectual curiosity. Nonetheless, monkey-wrench questioning would be an invaluable exercise for the vast majority of us, and it's simple. Just use this template:

I believe	
Because	
But how	
Why	
What if	

Your questions will need to be worded differently for each of your indoctrinated beliefs, but make sure you can ask and answer at least three probing questions for each belief. And, above all else, make sure your responses do not depend on other indoctrinated judgments and convictions.

The Courage To Commit – Apple is famous for its secrecy, but no product was kept under tighter wraps than the introduction of the iPhone. Scott Forstall who headed up development of Apple's iOS mobile operating system had to recruit a team of superstar engineers from around the company. His recruitment effort, however, was limited to this absurdly vague sales pitch:

> *We're starting a new project...It's so secret I can't even tell you what that project is. I can't tell you who you will work for...What I can tell you is that if you accept this project...you will work nights, you will work weekends, probably for a number of years.*

Take a moment to read Forstall's message again and consider how you would have responded. Would you have committed to a years-long project with the understanding that you wouldn't know what you'd be doing, who you were working with, or what rewards would await you at the completion of the project? And to top it off, you wouldn't be allowed to discuss the project with anyone else inside or outside of Apple. Some readers may scoff that this example is a no-brainer because of the reputation and prescient genius of Steve Jobs. We would disagree. Certainly the aura of Steve Jobs would affect one's decision to an extent, but the only people who would readily accept this kind of proposition are people who possess the kind of fearless open-mindedness that can only result from self-knowledge. People who are driven to achieve and enjoy pushing themselves to the limit. People who aren't afraid to make a decision and live with the results of that decision. People who know that there are no certainties in life. And most importantly, people who are choosing to live rather than simply preparing to live.

The Courage To Begin And End – Buddha said, "There are two mistakes one can make along the road to truth...not going all the way, and not starting." There is something inherent in the human spirit that causes us to fear both beginnings and endings. It's probably because both represent forks in the road, require a choice, and represent change. People tend to prefer the status quo with its attendant calmness and stability; but stasis, in regards to the human journey, implies existing rather than living. You may have heard the adage "sharks must keep swimming or they will die." It's an analogy that is frequently used by motivational speakers and management consultants to illustrate the human need for continual growth. In reality, the shark comparison is a false one as fewer than six percent of shark species actually need to swim in order to breathe. In regards to humans, however, the analogy does hold true. Every single one of us must indeed keep moving if we are to live to our fullest potential. But equally essential is the understanding that we must move in a series of starts and stops, zigs and zags. Our lives are not the journey of a speedboat that zooms ahead, never looks back, and leaves turmoil in its wake. Rather we are like a sailboat that must tack back and forth to progress and use the wind to full advantage. Every time we begin to zig we're making a conscious decision to stop zagging. There's no other way. We can't zig at the same time as we zag. Yet that is exactly how many people operate. They *really* want to zig but they also *really* don't want to stop zagging. The crux of the matter is that we're often afraid to zig because we don't know what it will mean or where it will lead; and we're afraid to stop zagging because we've invested so much time and effort in it. Plus we're not sure we're going to like zigging, so it would be much better to have zagging to fall back on. Of course none of this is about zigs and zags. It's about ending detrimental relationships and beginning new ones with hope and promise. Eliminating activities that don't add value and pursuing those that enrich your heart and mind. Knowing that quality trumps quantity and recognizing that having more is never enough. And most importantly, having the courage to never disappoint yourself in order to not disappoint someone else. (We realize this may sound selfish and confusing, but most of our fears regarding beginnings and endings revolve around others. The next paragraph and the concluding discussion of "locus of control" will provide further clarity.)

> **"There are two mistakes one can make along the road to truth...not going all the way, and not starting."**

The Courage To Say "I" – Selfishness has gotten a bad rap. There exists the wide-spread belief that we should always put others before ourselves, but

that view negates our unique individualism and diminishes the uniqueness we perceive and can nurture in others. "I" is a proclamation that we
know and like who we are. We are proud of our idiosyncrasies and refuse
to subjugate ourselves to the will of others. Our "I" is both current and
aspirational. It speaks to who we are today and what we expect to be in
the future. In truth, "I" is really all we can know. When we speak of "You"
we're interpreting you through a unique set of filters. When we speak of
"I" we can affirm the perspectives of both parties – e.g., "I respect what
you believe, but this is what I believe and here's why." Most critically, the
courageous act of acknowledging "I" ensures that we will take responsibility for our thoughts and actions, we will act decisively, we will stand by our
commitments, we will open our hearts and minds to wildly diverse ideas
and peoples, and we will recognize and celebrate that our "I" is part of a
much larger "We."

Locus Of Control

Fear, at its core, is about losing control – whether real or perceived. Some
of us have more control to lose than others. We each have a unique perspective on our place in the world – a place that can be measured via the
Locus of Control Scale. Developed in 1966 by Julian Rotter, a University
of Connecticut psychologist, the locus of control concept attempts to
measure the degree to which we believe our lives are determined in-
ternally by our own actions or externally by luck, the actions of others,
or the will of a God-like puppet-master of the universe. No one falls at
either extreme of the scale, and most of us share some attributes of both
internal and eternal controls. As a result we alternately feel all-powerful
and powerless.

In relation to fear and courage, individuals who score high on internal
control tend to possess a stronger sense of self-efficacy and, as a result, may
be less fearful about pursuing the "unknown." On the other hand, high internal control individuals may shy away from riskier endeavors because they
have only themselves to blame for any failures. Individuals with a strong
external locus of control perspective may feel they have no reason to push
themselves to achieve because the results are predetermined or otherwise
out of their hands.

20/20 Sight Line: Who's In Control?

Since being introduced by Dr. Rotter, the Locus of Control Scale has been studied, tested, and tweaked by dozens of psychologists. Many of these versions are available on the web for self-scoring. We would recommend trying two or three of the versions and see if your scores are consistent. Use this link to get started: **20-20MindSight.com/chapter8**

CHAPTER 9: *"A SUSPENSION OF LOGIC"*

Trust Your Gut

"You can't hit and think at the same time" is one of our favorite Yogi Berra quotes. His point is not that you can't do two things at once, but rather that you can sometimes over-think and hyper-analyze many activities and decisions. Oftentimes you have to act based on instinct and experience.

Call it what you want – a hunch, gut feeling, inner voice or "vibes" – but intuition is a universal, yet widely ignored and untapped, skill set. Unlike insight, which involves the rational transformation of information into knowledge and understanding, intuition is based on the unseen, nonverbal, and unconscious clues that surround us. Albert Einstein said, "I sometimes *feel* that I am right. I do not *know* that I am." The American writer Rita Mae Brown further described intuition as "a suspension of logic due to impatience." In a very real sense intuition is about knowing something without knowing how you know. In other words, intuitive *knowing* often hinges on the ability to see or feel patterns that others miss.

A classic example of how our subconscious mind can see and rapidly process patterns is the Japanese-invented method of "chicken sexing" – determining whether day-old hatchlings were male or female. Even the most expert "sexers" couldn't describe the visual clues that guided them. They knew they "saw" something but had no idea what that something was. As a result they couldn't systematically teach others how to identify males from females. Apprentice sexers learned the skill not by studying anatomy and reading textbooks but rather by observing the experts and imprinting the *invisible* clues onto their subconscious. These invisible clues turned into intuition.

In many circles intuition is a derogatory word because it operates outside the realms of science and quantifiable rationality. As a society, we've been taught to place our trust in conscious knowledge – empirical evidence that we can see and touch. Nonetheless, intuition has been the catalyst for innumerable "Aha!" moments ranging from the discoveries of Teflon, vulcanized rubber, and penicillin to Nobel prize-winning research in quantum physics. The English poet Robert Graves defines intuition as "the supra-logic that cuts out all the routine processes of thought and leaps straight from the problem to the answer." Using that definition, intuition can lead to new heights of achievement and personal fulfillment. As with all aspects of the human experience, intuition is part nature and part nurture.

Trust Your Gut

Chesley Sullenberger, the hero of US Air Flight 1549, said, "My decision to land in the Hudson was made thirty years ago." He had trained hard to become the best pilot possible and had rehearsed every possible scenario in simulations and in his mind. So when the moment arose, he made the decision quickly without consulting a spreadsheet of pros and cons. Up until that point, ninety-nine percent of his professional career could have been handled by any pilot of average ability. The same could be said about the careers of even the most acclaimed business geniuses – people like Ford's Allan Mulally and Virgin's Richard Branson. The key to their success was focused on the other one percent – the time when they needed to rely on their uniquely personal perspectives. They could see what others didn't. They were able to sort through the huge amount of information overload that we all contend with and distill it down to kernels of truth. They could turn experiential data into intuition, and the result was an ability to anticipate rather than react.

Their genius also hinged on knowing when to stop collecting data and make a damn decision. Former Secretary of State Colin Powell remarked that if he felt less than 40 percent confident about a decision, he'd stop and gather more information. Conversely, if his confidence level exceeded

70 percent, he'd reproach himself for wasting valuable time collecting too much data.

In a 1996 interview for *Wired* magazine, Steve Jobs boiled down intuition to the ability to connect and synthesize. "When you ask creative people how they did something, they feel a little guilty because they didn't really do it, they just saw something...they were able to connect experiences they've had and synthesize new things." We all do this to some degree. Sometimes we sense that something will happen before it occurs. We have immediate positive or negative feelings about a person or place based on no discernable facts. And we can tell when someone is holding back information or lying outright.

Gould's Facts And Darwin's Intuition

If you truly want to understand the value of an intuitive mindset, consider the case of Charles Darwin and John Gould. One is world renown while the other is a mere footnote in history. Here's the short version. Upon returning to London from his research journey to the Galapagos Islands, Darwin displayed the many specimens he had collected. The collection was examined by Britain's top naturalists many of whom – being scientists – relished the opportunity to point out errors made by their peers. John Gould, widely considered the greatest ornithologist of the time as well as an acclaimed author and artist, was one of the many naturalists that studied Darwin's trove. Gould quickly noted that Darwin had misidentified many of the bird specimens and, in fact, had collected thirteen distinct species of finches – the main variation among them being the shape of the beak. At this point, Gould's work was done; but Darwin's was just beginning.

Because intuition happens in the innermost recesses of the mind, Darwin's eureka moment was not immediate. It percolated as he considered Gould's findings and pondered why such an extraordinarily divergent variety of finches should exist. Over time Darwin realized that each type of finch was confined to a singular island and each finch's highly distinctive beak seemed to be ideally shaped for that island's environment and food source. Darwin's world-changing evolutionary theories based on natural selection emanated from that cause-and-effect realization. Darwin had Gould to thank for his epiphany moment, but Gould himself never endorsed Darwin's scientific conclusions. He remained an ardent creationist for the remainder of his life.

Today Darwin is a household name because he used intuition to extrapolate the theory of natural selection from a seemingly random series of facts. Gould, on the other hand, provided those selfsame facts but failed to see their significance or make the connective leap of faith. Gould believed that one-plus-one always equaled two. He was a highly educated man yet tended to consider facts as separate and discrete affirmations of the world he already knew and understood. Darwin had no such constraints. He let his mind synthesize facts and figures and combined it all with reflection and direct observation. If doing so led him to a place of unease – as the theory of evolution certainly did within his church and family – so be it. His genius was allowing his intellect – which was probably no greater than Gould's – to seek and to find. That genius resided within Darwin the whole time and it resides in all of us as well, waiting patiently to be freed from the shackles of conventional thinking.

20/20 Sight Line: Unleash Your Intuition

Intuition is highly correlated to decision-making, so one of the easiest ways to exercise and strengthen your intuition is to force yourself to make the commonplace decisions of daily life faster and without second-guessing. How long does it take you to decide what to order for lunch in a restaurant? How many times do you change your mind between first getting the menu and placing your order? And how many times do you end up ordering the same thing you always have? It may sound silly, but we hereby challenge you to limit your decision-making process to *10 seconds* when ordering from a menu, when deciding what color shirt to wear to work, when buying a new toothbrush, or when making any of the hundreds of other time-sucking decisions that have very little, if any, relevance to our happiness or fulfillment. Humor us and try this 10-second routine for a full week. If it doesn't work you can go back to agonizing over where to meet your friends on a Friday night or that everyday supermarket conundrum "paper or plastic?" If it does work you can pay it forward and recommend the exercise to friends and family.

Other writers and speakers recommend a variety of exercises to stoke your intuitive juices. Here are three of our go-to favorites:

- Have a handwritten debate with yourself, using one hand to argue Perspective A and the other hand to argue Perspective B. In theory, your non-dominant hand will write more subconsciously intuitive assertions. In practice, the very act of trying to write with your non-dominant hand forces you to use parts of your brain that are rarely called upon.

- Go simple. Part of the reason we tend to be so rational, rigid, and rules-based is that we're inundated with information that is uniformly rational, rigid, and rules-based. The trick is to distance yourself from the onslaught of data by doing something simple and absorbing – playing fetch with a dog, fishing, doing a jigsaw puzzle. Think about it this way, there is nothing in life simpler than taking a shower, yet that's where most people are at their creative best.

- Meditation is the most commonly prescribed technique to boost intuition, but we've found that even the idea of meditation is off-putting to many people. It sounds too New Age or crunchy. So forget about forcing yourself to "officially" meditate. Instead, find yourself a comfy chair. Turn off all lights, televisions, cell phones, and any other noise-emitting gadgetry. Then sit in the dark and let the quiet wash over you. It's like a shower without the water.

The bottom line is that you have an intuitive genius hiding somewhere inside you. It's eager to burst forth upon the scene but it's been kicked down so many times that it's understandably a little apprehensive. Treat it like a rescue puppy – give it love, respect, and a little space and it will return the favor many times over.

Please visit us at **20-20MindSight.com/chapter9** to download the worksheet, access new content, see how others have completed the exercise, and maybe share your results.

CHAPTER 10: *"MONOLOGUES IN THE PRESENCE OF A WITNESS"*

Stay In The Moment

Communication is a critical human skill. Accordingly, much of formal education is focused on reading and writing, with cursory attention given to oral presentation skills. Virtually no time, however, is spent on listening – which is why so many of us are poor listeners with minimal retention of what we hear. (The little instruction we do get often takes the form of "shut up and listen," a command that completely ignores the fact that listening involves much more than merely being quiet.) The writer Margaret Millar aptly defined most conversations between people as "simply monologues delivered in the presence of a witness."

The weird thing is that effective listening skills are inherent in humans. Infants are exemplars of listening. Aside from nursing and pooping, newborn babies do little other than listen. They can recognize voices they heard in the womb and they turn to see where sounds are coming from. They react to the type of sounds they hear – becoming excited when they hear animated voices and soothed when they hear whispers. And their reactions provide real-time feedback to whoever is speaking – e.g., "I like that," "make me giggle some more," or "I don't know about you but I think I need a time-out."

Some might argue that babies are naturally good listeners because their minds are blank slates. They're not weighed down by the baggage of life. They've never been hurt or disappointed. They're not judgmental. They love everything and everyone. None of those statements can be made about even the most righteous adult, but that does not detract from the simple power of infants to stay in the moment. And they do it by employing the three elements that are required for being present and accounted for in any dialogue or small-group discussion: active listening, focus, and mindfulness.

Listen Up

Hearing is to listening what eating is to digesting. True listening – active and engaged listening – is something you do with your entire being. You consciously invest time and attention to what the other person is saying, and you listen without filtering and prejudging. Active listening is contingent upon the suspension of disbelief, and it requires a thoughtful internal review of the information being presented before jumping to conclusions.

"Hearing is to listening what eating is to digesting."

As we stated at the beginning of this chapter, a big factor in why people don't listen effectively is that they've never been taught how to listen. But that excuse only goes so far. We all know exactly what active listening looks and feels like because it's what we expect others to do when we're talking – yet we rarely afford that courtesy to others.

The big question, then, is *why* don't we listen. The list of reasons could fill another book but let's start with the key activities we engage in instead of listening.

- *Rehearsing* – We think about what we're going to say.
- *Judging* – We give the proverbial thumbs-up or thumbs-down to the sentiments or arguments being stated.
- *Daydreaming* – We fantasize about all the other things we could be doing and sometimes check out the other person's clothing or hairstyle and wonder if they'd look better on us.
- *Mindreading* – We jump two miles ahead in the conversation and presume we know where the speaker is heading.
- *Scanning* – We know there's got to be someone in this room who's more interesting, important, or attractive than this chatterbox.

- *Placating* – We know this person means well but the only way to extricate ourselves is to nod and smile agreeably.

These listening-avoidance tactics are relatively benign. The real danger lies in the subconscious reasons for not listening.

- *We prefer listening to ourselves* – This is the big one. Why listen to someone else when our own dulcet tones are readily available?
- *We want to drive the conversation* – This is a subset of the previous bullet and points to the fact that in addition to wanting to hear ourselves we want to choose the topic.
- *We want to show we're smarter* – Why? Just because.
- *We're reluctant (and afraid) to change our opinions and beliefs* – There's nothing worse than having our social, political, and religious beliefs weakened or destroyed by a well-articulated counterargument. That's why conservatives watch Fox News and liberals watch MSNBC. We know we're right so why listen to the morons from the other side?

The reality of life is that we only learn when we listen. Whether in school, at work or in our communities, we don't learn by memorizing names, facts, and figures. We learn by understanding the context. By inferring. By interpreting what's not being said. And by sensing what can't be said. Some people might call this emotional intelligence or wisdom. We call it *20/20 Mind Sight.*

Actively Listen To Be Actively Heard

Jillian served on the board of a local non-profit and attended a strategic planning session facilitated by a well-known and highly regarded industry expert named Jay. She was eager to meet him and, when the day came, delighted that he exceeded her expectations. Here's why in her own words:

> *His presentation skills and knowledge were remarkable. He poked and prodded to elicit the depth of conversation necessary to iden-tify our core needs and establish a framework for a challenging yet*

realistic strategic plan. He interjected real-life anecdotes and high-lighted the tangible results that had been realized by other similar organizations.

I quite literally hung on his every word. I was scribbling notes as fast as I could, and I smiled, nodded, or shook my head at his insights and critiques. Keep in mind I was not consciously trying to behave this way. I was simply mesmerized by the content of his presentation and the authentic enthusiasm with which he delivered it.

After the session he came over to introduce himself. I had lots of questions for him – so many in fact that he asked if we could meet for coffee the following week to continue the discussion. When we met, the first thing he said was that I was paying such close attention to his presentation that it was almost distracting. He said he'd been speaking to groups for decades but he'd never seen anyone so engaged. He said he could feel my focus. I was embarrassed for a moment, but just for a moment. Then I owned it. I told him how important I believed it was to pay attention and be respectful. It provided an opportunity to share a win-win scenario: I'm helping you by listening and you're helping me by sharing your knowledge.

This anecdote would be powerful if it ended right there. But there's more. As a direct result of that single meeting over coffee, Jillian was invited to do a TEDx talk. This industry expert took the time to connect Jillian to the event director and gave a glowing endorsement. A few weeks later Jillian was on the TEDx stage sharing her presentation, "The Lens of Connectivity."

Get Focused

If you've jumped to the conclusion that "getting focused" means concentrating on a narrow sliver of information, you're partly right. That's the easy part of being focused. You've got one job to do. You eliminate all distractions and pay close attention to the task. Most people can do that for short stints, but that is not the type of focus we're talking about. The focus that's important is the ability to see – and to focus on – both the forest and the trees.

Think about it this way. You can focus with the narrow precision of a laser beam, the wider coverage of a flashlight, or the broad span of a floodlight. The more narrowly you focus, the more blind your eyes become to peripheral data points (which are often *not* peripheral in importance). The broader approach provides greater context and nuance – even if there remains a defined focal point.

The broader approach is also exponentially more difficult. The difficulty is that we're a society obsessed with achievement – with checking off items on our bucket lists. We've all experienced this when traveling in foreign countries. We see travelers glued to the viewfinder of a camera – trying to capture the perfect shot of the Eiffel Tower or the floating markets in Bangkok. They zoom in and out, try different angles, and force their kids to pose awkwardly next to the Beefeaters at the Tower of London. In the end they'll have a photographic record but no palpable memory of the moment or the experience.

Similarly, in our daily lives at home or work, we're always in a rush. We've got tons of paperwork, tight deadlines, and a visceral sense of being overwhelmed. To use a trite saying, we don't stop to smell the roses – or think about what we might be missing.

In her book *Rapt: Attention and the Focused Life* Winifred Gallagher insightfully summarizes the issue:

> *If you could look backward at your years thus far, you'd see that your life has been fashioned from what you've paid attention to and what you haven't. You'd observe that of the myriad sights and sounds, thoughts and feelings that you could have focused on, you selected a relative few, which became what you've confidently called "reality." You'd also be struck by the fact that if you had paid attention to other things, your reality and your life would be very different.*

In a very real sense, you decide what to focus on and what to ignore. It doesn't have to be like that. The world is rich and meant to be experienced in its totality. You will never experience that richness if you only focus on whatever shiny object happens to be dead center in your line of vision. Similarly, if you're fixated on what you have to do next you'll never experience the present. Which brings us to mindfulness.

Be Ever Mindful

The concept of mindfulness is often denigrated as new age psychobabble or a Buddhist-inspired approach to meditation. In its most basic and relevant form, however, mindfulness can help individuals stop fixating on themselves and more fully experience the connections with other people, with the world around them, and with every unique moment of their lives.

We live in a world where our daily activities are increasingly performed on autopilot. Think about your own situation. How many meals have you eaten without even tasting the food? How many times have you come to the end of a page in a book or magazine and realized you had no idea what you'd just read? How many times have you commuted to work and had no memory of anything between when you left your home and arrived at the office? The answer is probably way too many.

It's in that context where the practice of mindfulness and its primary tenets of "being in the moment" and "being present" can be invaluable. Truly fulfilled people don't live in the past or the future. They understand that the present is all we have. Regretting yesterday or hoping it were tomorrow isn't just a time-waster; it's a life-waster.

Countless books and articles have been written about mindfulness and its myriad benefits to body (physical), mind (neurological), and soul (spiritual). In all humility and with due respect to the reader, we are not experts in the multi-layered particulars of mindfulness in the fullest sense of the term. What we can offer, however, are some simple ways to incorporate mindfulness in your daily life:

- Be curious about all that you see and hear (and don't be afraid to ask questions)
- Be open to new ideas and people
- Eliminate the tendency to judge (quickly and superficially)
- Accept things as they are and move forward
- Change your routine – e.g., take a different route to work or shop at a different supermarket – and force yourself to pay attention

The Reverend Jesse Jackson shared this observation at a meeting about how to best motivate young people living in urban poverty: "The youth of today don't need our presents; they need our presence." The same can be true of everyone we meet. If we are present for them, they will be present for us; and we will all benefit from a mindful culture of shared learning, mutual respect, and a focus on the greater good.

> **"The youth of today don't need our presents; they need our presence."**

20/20 Sight Line: See For Yourself

Many people spend a majority of their time skimming over the surface of life. It's become so habitual that it's difficult to perceive in ourselves – but it's surprisingly easy to see in others.

Get yourself to a coffee shop or some other local venue where people congregate, sit together, and talk. Your 20/20 assignment is simply to observe. We're not trying to turn you into a creepy eavesdropper. In fact, the exercise is more effective when you can't hear what is being said. We just want you to observe.

Look closely at the facial expressions and body language as people converse. Pay particular attention to their eyes, head movements, and hands. What can you glean about the nature of the conversation? Is it all business, casual, or flirtatious? Is it cheerful or downbeat? Are both people equally engaged? Is one doing the majority of the talking? Are they making eye contact with each other, scanning the room, or checking their phones? Are they talking *to* or *at* each other? Do you think they'll remember this conversation the next day or will they forget it as soon as they get up to leave? Are they present for each other or just going through the motions?

As you observe these strangers try to apply the insights to your own personal interactions. How often do you "go through the motions" in order to seem polite – but without realizing that your lack of true presence is readily discernable and is among the rudest things you can do?

As Reverend Jackson observed, your presence is the most powerful gift you can bestow on others and on yourself.

Please visit us at **20-20MindSight.com/chapter10** to download the worksheet, access new content, see how others have completed the exercise, and maybe share your results.

CHAPTER 11: *"THERE IS NO CURE FOR CURIOSITY"*

Look Outside

D ale Carnegie said, "You can make more friends in two months by becoming interested in other people than you can in two years by trying to get other people interested in you." Carnegie speaks to the dichotomy that most people want to be viewed as interesting, yet a surprisingly small percentage of us are truly interested in others or the world at large. Individuals who commit themselves to building a 20/20 worldview, on the other hand, are curiosity freaks. They are junkies for meeting new people, building diverse relationships, and searching for knowledge regardless of how far afield those people, relationships, and knowledge may be from their traditional social milieu and professional stomping grounds.

> *"You can make more friends in two months*
> *by becoming interested in other people*
> *than you can in two years by trying to*
> *get other people interested in you."*

We live in a time of specialization in which people focus on expanding their expertise in increasingly narrow niches. There is widespread and derisive disdain for anyone who aspires to being a "jack of all trades and master of none." This perspective has lead to a decades-long surge in "trade-related" college majors like finance and accounting along with a not-coincidental decrease and devaluation of liberal arts degrees. Education is viewed as a means to an end – a high-paying job with a big title and an equally big office. College students choose courses and internships that will enhance their resumes with little thought to broadening their knowledge base and worldview. Interestingly, one of the most successful and insightful business minds of the last century took a decidedly different approach to his own education. Steve Jobs, Apple's founder and mastermind, famously praised an audited calligraphy course as the inspiration for the WYSIWYG – what-you-see-is-what-you-get – interface of the original Macintosh computer. In today's MBA or undergraduate business programs a calligraphy class or any other soft-skill curriculum would never qualify as admissible credits; yet Jobs believed that single course changed the history of computing. The moral is that pursuing knowledge outside your core competencies can significantly boost your personal and professional life competencies.

An equally significant downside in focusing on the familiar is the constraint it places on our social circles. The majority of people maintain friendships with people just like themselves. Part of that is because we tend to live and work with people similar to ourselves. That means we have to make an extra effort to initiate and nurture relationships with people outside our usual personal and professional spheres. Doing that is quite easy – but few people think about it on a daily basis. And if you don't think about it, you won't fix it. That's why you often see speaker panels at industry and association conferences composed entirely of white males. (The most famous example occurred in the U.S. House of Representatives when an all-male committee convened to discuss the female reproductive system.) Conference planners don't consciously choose homogeneity, nor do they purposely choose to ignore diverse participants or exclude the wide range of differing viewpoints that would naturally result from a broader panel. It simply never enters their mind.

So when we say it's easy to expand our social and professional circles, we really mean it. It's like riding a bike. It looks scary and difficult until you try it and become hooked for life. You just have to hop on and trust yourself and the people around you.

Put Your Interest On Display
Curiosity is an activity not a passive state of mind. It's not enough to say or believe you're interested in the outside world; you need to exude your interest. Here's how to do it in three simple steps.

- Share a Smile – Like yawns, smiles are contagious; and it's well known that people can literally hear a smile over the phone. What's dumbfounding is how rarely people actually smile. That's especially true around people we don't know very well, but it's also true of our day-to-day interactions with family, friends, and colleagues. What's sadly ironic is that smiles can energize, relax, and empower both the "smiler" and the "smilee." The very act of smiling shifts our focus onto the "target" and in turn dramatically affects the way others see us and engage with us. Smiles radiate energy and generate interactions that would otherwise have been ignored or overlooked.

- Look'em in the Eye – It sounds simple and commonsensical but eye contact will unequivocally separate you from the crowd. Eye contact represents both a request and an invitation – a knock on the door of the other person's world and a welcoming invitation to enter yours. The old saying that the eyes are the windows to the soul became a cliché because it contains so much truth. Our eyes reveal our genuine feelings. Eyes can signal trust, honesty, fear, engagement, warmth, love, disdain, dismay, and pretty much every other emotion you can name. Our eyes are powerful tools – but only if we use them.

- Keep in Touch – Several years ago Jillian was working at a private invite-only event for the who's who in the Boston business and financial community. Her role was "to do what she does" – i.e., meet as many people as possible, make introductions, identify and create opportunities, and crack the shell of detachment that most meeting attendees construct (consciously or not). One such person was "Charles" who introduced himself as an investment banker. He elaborated a bit further and then Jillian looked him smack in the eyes and, with a half-joking tone, remarked, "Wow, how nice. Now let's talk about something a bit more exciting. Tell me a fun fact about yourself." Charles was a bit taken aback and then a smile stretched across his face. He exhaled deeply and began to talk about his love of music. That led the conversation to his children and the instruments they play. He was becoming human and Jillian was able to connect in a more engaging and substantive way. A month later Jillian ran into Charles again at another executive networking event, and she knew exactly how to kick off the conversation. In Jillian's words:

> I asked if he'd recorded any new hits since I'd last seen him or if he'd gone to any cool shows. In an instant we were long-term friends and the conversation flowed. I also learned one new important detail: the harmonica was his favorite instrument. A couple of months later I was visiting a client's store and noticed a jar of mini-harmonicas at the register. Charles came to mind and I bought him one. I wrote a card and enclosed the harmonica. On the outside of the envelope I wrote something like this: Now you can keep your music with you anywhere you go. I mailed it off with a huge grin thinking about how he would react when seeing it. Fast-forward a couple of months to when I get a frantic call from Charles. He was rattling on about how sorry he was and that I must think he was a jackass for not acknowledging the gift. He told me it was the single best gift he'd ever received. He explained that the delay was due to his company's relocation and the resulting backup in the forwarding of some packages. Then he began playing a few notes on his mini-harmonica. This big, bad, important investment banker was presenting himself to me in the most human of ways with pure joy and almost childlike enthusiasm. I was beyond thrilled because this was exactly why I'd sent the gift: I simply wanted to make him smile and let him know I was thinking about him. Period.

But that wasn't the end of it. Shortly afterward, Charles met with Jillian to discuss a new initiative. Over coffee he invited her to serve as a founding member and strategic consultant for a just-formed CEO group.

So let's give it a whirl. Next time you head out take a moment to think about something that makes you so happy you just have to smile. Hold that smile and see what happens when you practice the one-two punch of smiling and eye contact. In particular notice the change in your own attitude and posture. We guarantee you'll be standing straighter and walking with a bounce in your step. And you'll notice the same positive vibes being returned by everyone you meet. Keep doing this until it becomes second nature, and you'll soon begin meeting more diverse people and having more fascinating conversations than you ever thought possible. All of which will further whet your interest in the world around you.

"Curiosity is an activity not a passive state of mind."

Share Your Ignorance

In addition to building connections via interest in others, the 20/20 approach encourages individuals to stand out by professing their ignorance rather than trying to demonstrate how smart they are. Peter Drucker was once asked by a student for the secret to his success in advising companies. Drucker's response was that there was no secret: "You just need to ask the right questions." He continued with this insight: "You must frequently approach problems with your ignorance; not what you think you know from past experience because, not infrequently, what you think you know is wrong." The bottom line is that questioning born out of genuine interest is the most direct path to true understanding.

But interest itself is not enough. Think back and consider how many times in your own life you chose to sit back and not ask a "stupid" question. Most likely it was a legitimate question that needed to be asked and one whose response you truly wanted to hear, but you held back because you didn't want to display your ignorance of the subject. You didn't want to be embarrassed in front of your boss or look silly in front of a loved one. But if you really look back at those moments, and really be honest with yourself, you can probably identify several other people who were dying to ask the same question but were also afraid to ask. And if you look back to the aftermath of that particular situation you'll probably see how the process or result would have been improved if someone had asked that stupid question.

"Questioning born out of genuine interest is the most direct path to true understanding."

Look Outside Yourself

What subject do people love talking about more than any other? Themselves. And that's the Catch 22 of establishing and maintaining strong interpersonal relationships. We want to talk about ourselves but everyone we talk to wants the discussion to be about them. It's a pervasive problem but one that is remedied by simply putting yourself in the other person's shoes and understanding what she sees and hears.

A good conversationalist is not one who makes himself feel better but rather someone who makes other people feel better. And doing so ain't rocket science. In fact the solution was provided in *Martine's Handbook of Etiquette, and Guide to True Politeness* written by Arthur Martine in 1866. Martine observed that most people are ineffective and ill-mannered in everyday discourse, and he identifies eight archetypes that presume "I" am here to speak and "You" are here to listen:

- The *loud bore* who "allows no one else to utter a word."
- The too-much-information *life-sharing bore* who assumes "Whatever is his must...interest others."
- The *clever bore* who "cannot allow the simplest conversation to go on, without entering into proofs and details familiar to every child nine years of age."
- The *apathetic bore* who affects "a total indifference to the party present, and to the subject of discourse."
- The *lingering bore* who simply cannot believe you can exist without his presence.
- The *one-trick pony bore* who "constantly speaks on the same eternal subject."
- The *malaprops bore* who possesses a "special gift for choosing the least appropriate topics of conversation, [e.g.] To the blind they will speak of fine pictures and scenery."
- The *egotistical bore* who is always ready "to slime over every subject of discourse with the vile saliva of selfish vanity."

Later in the book Martine offers a delightful summation of the key attributes of artful and effective conversation which – if internalized – will gracefully open the doors to more and deeper relationships than you ever thought possible.

> Cheerfulness, unaffected cheerfulness, a sincere desire to please and be pleased, unchecked by any efforts to shine, are the qualities you must bring with you into society, if you wish to succeed in conversation. ... a light and airy equanimity of temper ... that spirit which never rises to boisterousness, and never sinks to immovable dullness; that moves gracefully from "grave to gay, from serious to serene," and by mere manner gives proof of a feeling heart and generous mind.

Read this section again and see if any of it sounds like you. Are you letting people know you're genuinely interested in hearing about them? Are you continually interrupting and changing the subject to bring it back to your own interests? Are you trying to impress others with your intellect or are you hoping to be impressed by others? Are you expending more energy on being interesting or are you focused on being interested?

Unleash Your Inner Child

Many great minds ranging from Goethe to Edison to Hawking have underscored the belief that the human search for meaning and answers – i.e., intellectual growth and self-improvement – was critical to personal fulfillment. None has stated it as concisely as the American writer Dorothy Parker: "The cure for boredom is curiosity. There is no cure for curiosity." Interest in the world at-large is the linchpin of a fully realized life. We live in a fascinating world during fascinating times yet many people show little curiosity beyond their self-defined boundaries. That is no way to live.

> ### "The cure for boredom is curiosity.
> ### There is no cure for curiosity."

Think about the most joyous people you know. Odds are that you would describe them as "full of life," and we would bet the house that they are always learning, meeting new and interesting people, and doing unusual and fun things. If it didn't sound so derogatory and demeaning, you might even suggest that they possess a child-like innocence and a wide-eyed curiosity for the world around them.

Children gleefully savor moments that their older and more mature counterparts dismiss as mundane – if they notice them at all. Many adults seem to believe that an air of indifference suggests a certain sophistication and worldliness. They foster a been-there-done-that attitude and would rather remain ignorant than confess unfamiliarity with the topic or issue. Part of it is ego and part is laziness. The more you know the more powerful you appear. Conversely, admitting your ignorance knocks you several rungs down on the social and professional ladder.

It can be hard work to embrace your curiosity, learn a new skill, acquire new information that threatens deeply held beliefs, or connect with some-one who shatters every stereotype about what being Black/Muslim/gay/Latino/disabled/etc. is "supposed to be like." So, yes it's hard work, but to play off of the Dale Carnegie quote that opened this chapter:

> ## "The more interested you are, the more interesting you become."

20/20 Sight Line: Give Yourself Five

So if the "cure" for curiosity is to look outside yourself, let's see how well you're doing. Please write – and it's important to write these down rather than just think about them – your response to the following.

- Name five things you did for the first time over the last year.
- Name five people who you now consider friends that you met for the first time over the last year.

Were you able to identify any activities or friendships that were initi-ated over the last year? Many people score a big goose egg on this exercise so don't fret if you're in that category. You've got another year ahead of you to make amends and expand your horizons, but it won't happen without a written plan and specific goals. To wit:

- Name five things you will do for the first time over the next year.
- Name five opportunities to meet new people that you'll take advantage of over the next year.

Please visit us at **20-20MindSight.com/chapter11** to download the worksheet, access new content, see how others have completed the exercise, and maybe share your results.

CHAPTER 12: *"A LIFETIME OCCUPATION"*

Want More (Of The Right Stuff)

**"Ambition is good; selfishness is bad; and the
line between the two is gossamer thin."**

Everyone in the world desires more, but there are two distinct types of desire. There are people who want more simply to have more, and there are those who want more in order to be more. The former are in competition with friends and colleagues to see who can make the most money, have the biggest house, and die with the most toys. These are the selfish ones. The latter are on a quest for knowledge, achievement, and experience which, when combined, turn into wisdom, selfless generosity, and a focus on the greater good. These are the ambitious ones.

Mother Teresa was ambitious, as were Aristotle, Thomas Jefferson, and Pablo Picasso – and they all left the world a better place than when they arrived. Picasso himself once said, "I am always doing that which I cannot do, in order that I may learn how to do it." That's an ambition born of an aspirational orientation rather than a material focus.

Which type of desire describes you – having more or being more? Money or meaningfulness? It's an important question that will define your core character and guide your 20/20 journey. Are you in it for wealth, fame, and glory; or do you seek fulfillment and personal satisfaction?

Before you answer that question, ask yourself this: "Are the two types of desire mutually exclusive?" Our response is that almost nothing in life is totally black and white. Even the most selflessly ambitious of us still experience a prideful buzz and deep-seated feelings of gratification as our achievements multiply and attract interest from those around us. The key demarcation between being more and having more is this: Would you continue to do more to be more even if it wouldn't lead to having more? If the answer is yes, your ambition exerts a positive influence on your life and community. On the flipside, if you would do pretty much anything in order to have more, you've begun a downward spiral that may ultimately leave nothing but hurt, damage, and emptiness in its wake.

> ***"I am always doing that which I cannot do,***
> ***in order that I may learn how to do it."***

An Itch For Learning

A critical component of the 20/20 mindset is the quest for knowledge via a lifetime of continual learning. Learning is not something that only occurs when you're young or when you're inside the walls of an academic institution. It occurs when you read or observe, when you listen, when you pay attention, and when you question. It occurs in the shower, while driving or walking the dogs. You just have to be ready for it. Open to new ideas that challenge old ones. Willing to see what others ignore. And proud to think for yourself and say the things that others repress.

Learning is not something that is done to you. It's something you participate in. Indeed, one of the best ways to learn is to teach. That doesn't mean you have to actually stand up in front of a classroom. It means you need to share your knowledge with others in order to gain more knowledge. Sharing knowledge with co-workers and friends creates a *quid pro quo* situation where they'll want to repay you with specialized knowledge of their own. In addition the act of teaching – whether explaining something verbally or demonstrating it physically – serves to affirm and reinforce the lesson (concept, shortcut, methodology, etc.) in your own mind. Teaching what you know, and seeing how others respond, can also prompt you to reconsider and refine your own knowledge base. In turn, sharing knowledge will make you smarter and a better teacher.

Much has been written of the "Learning Organization," but little import has been afforded the "Learning Mindset." As a result most of us don't think about how we learn or actively seek opportunities to learn. Some of us even have the view that our knowledge is fixed or that there is a limit to how much we can actually learn and assimilate. Neurologists will tell you there's much about the brain that science does not fully understand. The medical journals frequently feature major disagreements over the causality and functioning of synapses and neurotransmitters. The one thing they all agree on is that humans have only began to tap into the full power of the brain. There is probably a limit on how much the brain can process and store, but even geniuses like Albert Einstein and Stephen Hawking haven't gotten close to maxing out their gray matter. Which means the rest of us have inter-cranial hard drives that are barely spinning.

Laurels Make An Uncomfortable Resting Spot

Way back in the seventeenth century, Queen Christina of Sweden said, "It is necessary to try to surpass one's self always; this occupation ought to last as long as life." From the 20/20 perspective, life's journey must always be moving forward. This may sound like commonsense bordering on psychobabble nonsense but the concept of forward movement is foreign to many people and downright scary to many others. Isaac Newton's law of inertia explains that an object in motion tends to stay in motion, while an object at rest tends to stay at rest. In today's world, and probably throughout human history, inertia is the predominant state. Which is why it's so surprising when we encounter people who refuse to rest on their laurels. These individuals tend to be highly reflective and high achieving, and they focus on what's next not what's already been done. Best of all, they combine that focus with a genuine sense of urgency.

We realize that sports analogies are grossly over used, but sometimes nothing else works quite as well. That's especially true regarding the achievement of your full potential. Here's an example. When Randy Moss first joined the New England Patriots in 2007 he remarked how impressed he was with Tom Brady's work ethic. Moss said that if you were watching a team practice and didn't know better, you would think Brady was desperately trying to make the team and not get cut. At this point in his career, Brady had led his team to three Super Bowl championships, multiple Pro Bowl appearances, and numerous passing and post-season victory records. But he still had the itch. He wasn't satisfied. He felt he could do more and his team could accomplish more. He understood that football was a team sport, and he was willing to make personal sacrifices to make the team stronger. While we doubt there has ever been a corporate CEO who willingly reduced his pay in order to surround himself with the best possible talent, Brady has repeatedly renegotiated his contract to free up money to pay for quality receivers, linemen, and defensive backs. That's akin to a CEO lowering his salary to attract a top-quality comptroller, general counsel, or human resources executive. It doesn't happen because most CEOs get their jollies from money rather than corporate performance.

Continuing the sports analogy, no one ever tries out for a sports team to be a benchwarmer. Everyone wants to be a starter. That's why elite athletes play just as hard during practice as they do in an actual game. Elite athletes know they can only improve by pushing themselves. Non-elite athletes are decidedly less determined. Some just go through the motions in practice, doing just enough to ward off the coach's admonishments. Others work like hell when they're trying to make the team only to ease off when they've hit the big time. We can all name high-profile professional athletes who sign big contracts following a career-year and never play the same again. They were in it for the money – to make more rather than be more – and once the money was banked there was nothing else to play for. Tom Brady has banked all the money any human could ever want or need, but he's still playing his heart out on the practice field and on game days.

You can do the same. Approach every day as a tryout where you're trying to impress the coach with your skills, intelligence, and dedication. Stop sitting in your cubicle waiting for an assignment; design one. Don't wonder whether the cute barista at the local Starbucks would like to go out for dinner with you; ask him. Don't stay at a meaningless job that you hate; find one that delivers meaning and joy. Don't say yes just because it's easier; stand up for yourself.

Inertia refers to a physical law of nature, but it is equally a psychological phenomenon.

"It is necessary to try to surpass one's self always; this occupation ought to last as long as life."

The Ten Million Dollar Question

Answer these questions honestly and specifically:

- What would you do if you won ten million dollars?
- Would your life change?
- Would you change?
- If so, how? And why?
- How would you spend your time?
- What would you be itchy for if money were no longer a concern?

Those questions will help identify your aspirational itch that's desperate to be scratched. In addition, if you take time to seriously reflect on your responses, they will point out the folly of waiting around to win the lottery before pursuing your passions. Waiting is an insidious form of inertia. Waiting for something to happen before you pursue your dreams hands over the reins of your life to an external force. It's an admission that you are not in control of your life, and we can't think of a more disheartening admission and more strident disavowal of the power of the human mind.

"Waiting is an insidious form of inertia."

Waiting for some external event also provides a convenient excuse for tacit acceptance of what Thoreau described as "lives of quiet desperation." Each of us has the ability to change our lives for the better by embracing our passions and nurturing our interests. It's not an all-or-nothing scenario. We're not suggesting you quit your day-to-day job to pursue your dream of being a writer of romance novels, a backyard farmer growing thousand-pound pumpkins, or the creator of the next life-changing iPhone app. What we are suggesting is that you can put aside an hour or two every day to focus on an activity that brings you joy and provides a taste of what it would be like to be awarded ten million dollars.

(We feel compelled to stress that no amount of money will necessarily transform someone's life from dreary to transcendent. Money does not lead to a fulfilling life. There are countless multi-millionaires who live passionless lives, while their lower income counterparts are satisfied with every aspect of their lives and wouldn't change a thing if they came into money.)

Two thousand years ago, the Roman philosopher Seneca wrote a timeless treatise, *On the Shortness of Life*, in which he observed, "It is not that we have a short time to live, but that we waste a lot of it...Life is long if you know how to use it." Seneca would enthusiastically endorse our suggestion to pursue passion-related activities *today* rather than waiting for serendipity to intercede. In fact, he did: "Putting things off is the biggest waste of life; it snatches away each day as it comes, and denies us the present by promising the future. The greatest obstacle to living is expectancy, which hangs upon tomorrow and loses today."

"Life is long if you know how to use it."

Write It Down To Scratch The Itch

One of Phil's favorite assignments is having students write personal mission statements about what they want to accomplish in both the short- and long-term. We strongly urge every reader of this book to do the same. There is a special magic about writing things down. It's a contemplative process that forces you to really think about the subject and internalize the insights and perspectives gleaned from purposeful thinking.

Over the years Phil has loved reading what these young men and women see themselves accomplishing in the years ahead. Most of them get very specific about their aspirations and name the company they want to be with, the kind of job they want to hold, when they expect to marry and have children, and where they will live. Others paint broader pictures including one student who wrote this: "Over the next five years I want to have an opinion and actually know what I am talking about. I want to learn something new every day and read at least one new book every month. In five years I want to have read every play by William Shakespeare. And over the next 10 years I want to become an expert in something." That sentiment perfectly exemplifies the kind of ambition that accompanies self-knowledge and leads to personal fulfillment.

Whether you choose to provide granular-level detail about your mission or take a wide-angle approach, the very act of thinking about and writing a mission statement will help ensure that you recognize what you're itchy for and get focused on how best to scratch it.

20/20 Sight Line: "20 Years From Now"

As a starting point towards formulating your lifetime mission statement, please use the following template to map out your goals along with the tactics you'll employ to achieve those goals. We've used a 20-year horizon, but you can use any time frame that works best for you. Or create multiple game plans – a 5-year plan, a 20-year plan, and a 40-year plan.

Please visit us at **20-20MindSight.com/chapter12** to download the worksheet, access new content, see how others have completed the exercise, and maybe share your results.

My 20 Year Game Plan

Today in 2036, I can look back on my life and see that I had a clear picture of what I wanted to achieve. I recognized my personal strenghts and weaknesses. And I realize that, unless I began to know my self and focus my efforts, I would never achieve all that I was capable of.

From the very outset, my personal and professional life was fashioned after the template of my personal vision and a deep understanding of my character. And each and every day I attempted to model my self after that template. At the end of each day, I would ask myself how well I had done, and discovered the disparity between where I was and where I had committed myself to be. At the start of the following day, I set out to make up for the difference. And it all started way back when I completed this simple exercise:

Twenty years from now, I will have achieved all that I am capable of for three special and specific reasons. The first reason is that, starting today, I will

_____

_____

_____

The second reason is that I recognize that _____
is my greatest and most valuable personal strength and I will utilize, continually enhance, and leverage that strength by _____

_____

_____

_____

The third reason I will have been so successful is that I recognize that my area of weakness - and the greatest threat to my success - is _____
and I will do the following to mitigate, eliminate or compensate for that weakness

_____

_____

_____

Signed and Attested on ___ /___ /_____ : _____

CHAPTER 13: *"NOTHING INTELLIGENT"*

Act Up

There's a great scene in the quirky movie *Benny and Joon* where one character, Sam, is in a local park entertaining Benny, Joon, and a crowd of onlookers with a Charlie Chaplin-like vaudeville routine. After a round of applause from the crowd, Benny turns to Sam.

"That was great," he says. "Did you learn that in school?"

"No," replies Sam. "I was kicked out of school for that."

Sam's experience is common to most people. From a very young age we've been warned about the dangers of acting up, being silly, or otherwise not conforming to the policies, procedures, and norms of the institutions and people around us. Far from being a danger, however, these instances of "acting up" often serve as the catalyst for innovation, creativity, and true insight. Think about it this way: as computers become increasingly intelligent and outperform humans on a wide range of tasks, the one thing computers can't do is have fun, take directionless flights of fancy, and allow their On/Off imaginations to soar. That's where people shine, so why would anyone consider shutting down the imaginative process? The reasons are varied and complex but boil down to one simple explanation: anxiety. We're afraid of not being taken seriously. Of being dismissed as a lightweight or being eliminated from consideration for a position of greater responsibility and authority. Of allowing our considerable subconscious brainpower to explore thoughts and feelings far beyond the purview of our day-to-day activities – thoughts and feelings that might run counter to what we think we believe. In short we're afraid to broaden our perspective because of where it might lead. We're afraid that opening our hearts and minds to a different approach to living and thinking could result in a life-altering epiphany from which there is no going back. To the 20/20 mindset that possibility sounds exciting; to others it approaches pure terror.

Playfulness

Ludwig Wittgenstein said, "If people never did silly things, nothing intelligent would ever get done." And rather than viewing playfulness as a sign of immaturity, Abraham Maslow believed, "The most mature people are the ones that can have the most fun...These are people who can regress at will, who can become childish and play with children and be close to them." A key tenet of the 20/20 mindset is that playfulness is not pointless but rather a manifestation of unbridled delight that serves as a powerful springboard to imaginative brainstorms and creative thinking.

> *"The most mature people are the ones*
> *that can have the most fun."*

Our academic and corporate institutions are conventional by nature, but they do a grave disservice by mandating a similar perspective among their students and employees. Convention focuses on the empirical, the tried-and-true, and the practical – all of which are mortal enemies of inspiration and innovation. Convention takes joy only in objects specifically designed to provide joy rather than creating joy from the inside out. Children suffer from no such myopia. Give them lemons and they won't make lemonade because that would be too simple and trite. Instead, they might play a game of lemon bocce or bowling. Maybe they'll juggle them and see who can keep them in the air the longest. Maybe they'll squirt the juice into their mouths and see who can swallow without scrunching up their faces. Or maybe they'll try to balance the lemons on their heads, or cut them in halves and make believe they're overturned turtles that need to be saved, or quarter them and see if they'll float in the bathtub like an armada of yellow battleships.

Kids do this all the time. Give toddlers a wrapped present and it's a safe bet they'll spend more time playing with the wrapping paper and the box than the gift itself. They do this with no particular agenda or purpose;

it's just what they do. They get lost in the moment, totally mesmerized by this tactile and cerebral activity. It's unguarded, exciting, and energizing (to themselves as well as any onlookers). It's how they experience life – at least until they're told to stop acting like a baby and making a mess.

If you're human, you've been told at some point in your life to grow up and act your age. The translation is that it's time to stop having fun and get more serious. Life is F-ing serious, after all, and if you want to make something of yourself you need to frown far more than you smile. That's what we've been taught, but it's a lie.

Research at Penn State has demonstrated that playfulness is a key determinant in one's attractiveness to the opposite sex (or, presumably, to the same sex if one is gay). Other studies have concluded that playfulness in adults is positively correlated to academic performance, a predisposition to innovate and experiment, high self-esteem, and the creation of happier and more satisfying interpersonal relationships.

The truth is that there's no downside to maintaining a playful attitude throughout life (aside from those circumstances in which a certain decorum is de rigueur). Let your inner child shine brightly on anyone who crosses your path, and you yourself will shine brighter than you ever have before.

Laugh Out Loud

Most people know that yawns are contagious, but few realize that smiles and laughter are equally infectious.

It's hard not to smile back at someone who smiles at you. Try it sometime and we'd bet it makes you feel foolish and small. The bigger issue of course is why anyone would choose to not reciprocate a smile. Smiles create connections, even if they're fleeting. Smiles are an acknowledgement that we're all the same regardless of our differences. Smiles are kind and generous.

The sight and sound of laughter will similarly engender more laughter. Laughing is fun on its own, but it also provides a wide range of physical and psychological benefits. Laughter can relieve anxiety, reduce stress, enhance mood by releasing endorphins, and contribute to a more positive outlook on life. And shared laughter is how relationships begin and grow stronger.

"Smiles are an acknowledgement that we're all the same regardless of our differences."

Smiling and laughing are the ultimate win-win human activities. That's why silly cat videos are so popular on social media. We need laughter in our lives and we actively seek opportunities to experience it – and when found, we actively share it with friends and family. That's certainly a good thing, but it could be even better. Instead of looking outside for smile opportunities, create your own. To wit:

Ten Things You Can't Do Without Smiling and/or Laughing

- Playing with puppies (or dogs) and kittens (or cats)
- Licking an ice cream cone (especially on a hot day when you're racing against the clock to stop it from melting all over your face and hands)
- Riding a go-cart
- Having a Super-Soaker battle
- Juggling (and learning to juggle)
- Playing charades
- Watching a toddler do something – anything – for the first time
- Finger-painting
- Writing a limerick
- Identifying ten things you can't do without smiling and/or laughing

Use Uncommon Sense

Before Sarah Palin exploded on the political scene in 2008 and subsequently imploded as a mean-spirited, self-centered airhead, the term "maverick" meant something specific and noteworthy. Mavericks were independent-minded individuals who refused to bow to the conventional wisdom of the masses. They understood that common sense was a constraint. And because they were driven by the power of their beliefs, they possessed thick skin to fend off the arrows that were invariably slung at those who presumed to live or think differently.

At one point in their lives, many geniuses – from Galileo to Edison to Elon Musk – have been derided as delusional, unrealistic, and maniacal quacks for their "foolish" pursuits. It didn't stop them and it shouldn't stop you. If you think like everyone else, you'll forever be held back by the armies of sycophants and naysayers who are content with leaving things just the way they are. This poem, "It Can Be Done," was included in *The Children's Book of Virtues* edited by William J. Bennett. It's a testament to the power of guiding your life by the light of your personal vision.

"It Can Be Done"
The man who misses all the fun
Is he who says "it can't be done."
In solemn pride he stands aloof
And greets each venture with reproof.
Had he the power he'd efface
The history of the human race;
We'd have no radio or motor cars,
No streets lit by electric stars
No telegraph nor telephone,
We'd linger in the age of stone.
The world would sleep if things were run
By men who say, "It can't be done."

Among Apple's most memorable advertising campaigns was the 1997 "Think Different" series. The ads featured black-and-white photographs of famous mavericks ranging from Bob Dylan and Mahatma Gandhi to Muhammad Ali and Pablo Picasso. The campaign was dedicated to the crazy ones:

> *The ones who see things differently.*
> *They're not fond of rules. And they have no respect for the status quo. You can quote them, disagree with them, glorify or vilify them.*
> *About the only thing you can't do is ignore them. Because they change things. They invent. They imagine. They heal. They explore. They create. They inspire. They push the human race forward.*
> *Maybe they have to be crazy.*

When was the last time you were a little crazy? A time when you *allowed* yourself to be a little crazy? Many of us are buttoned up so tightly that common sense, conventional wisdom, and groupthink are the only concepts we hold sacred. They allow us to feel safe and mitigate our fears. But there can be no question that they also hold us back from achieving our full potential. If we cannot separate ourselves from the crowd then we are forever doomed to being just another face in the crowd.

If we can instead embrace uncommon sense, acknowledge our idiosyncrasies, and celebrate our unique perspective on the world, our voices can add richness and diversity to every conversation. You will learn and grow – and you'll help others learn and grow.

20/20 Sight Line: Entertain Yourself

This entire book is focused on personal reflection and self-knowledge and that same approach works well in regard to "Acting Up" in your own life. Think about your day-to-day activities and articulate how you do – or how you can – incorporate some silliness into the routine. Silliness that serves two purposes: delivering moments of joy and reaffirming your personal brand and perspective on life. To get you started, Jillian and Phil are publicly sharing three ways they get a daily dose of the sillies.

Jillian:

- I'm big on exchanging high-fives with people "just because." As high-fives are typically celebratory, offering a high-five for no particular reason is a fun way to say hello; and it elicits a smile and sense of micro-community 99.9% of the time.
- I love to make up absurd lyrics to the tune of well-known songs. And as a corollary, I will often insert song lyrics or movie lines to see if the person I'm speaking with catches on.
- I have been known to break out dance moves in public settings like the pharmacy, grocery store, or Home Depot when a good tune comes on – and I love when someone catches me doing it and joins in.

Phil:

- Despite having the worst singing voice in the history of humankind, I love to break out into opera-mode and infuse the most mundane verbal interactions – "Pass the butter please" – with joyous passion.
- All the females in my life share the same middle name – Marie. It began with my wife and daughter and continues with our Labrador retrievers: Ruby Marie, Riley Marie, and Maisy Marie.
- As the owner of a Jeep Wrangler, I'm always on the lookout for other Wrangler drivers in order to share the Jeep Wave. The other owner might be diametrically opposed to everything I believe in, but for that moment in time we're simpatico brothers (or brother and sister). It's a fun and silly tradition that I embrace and cherish.

Now let's see yours.

-
-
-

Please visit us at **20-20MindSight.com/chapter13** to download the worksheet, access new content, see how others have completed the exercise, and maybe share your results.

CHAPTER 14: *"WHEN NOBODY LIKES YOU"*

Lead By Example

n *The Great Gatsby*, Nick Carraway observes that Gatsby regards him with "an incredible prejudice in my favor." Despite being younger and far less accomplished than his mentor, Carraway felt that Gatsby needed, respected, and valued him. It was not a one-way street. The two men shared a deep emotional connection and Gatsby benefitted from their relationship just as much as Carraway. While we would never offer Gatsby as an exemplar of human beneficence, he had an innate ability to inspire and motivate and he possessed a masterful understanding of the nuances of micro-messaging. Gatsby created a dynamic with Carraway that was welcoming and inclusive. The words Gatsby used when speaking with Carraway were certainly important, but far more critical were the non-verbal and paralinguistic affirmations of their relationship – things like body language, facial expressions, physical proximity and contact, vocal tone and inflection, and active listening. Much of this happens unconsciously, but it is a direct outgrowth of a mindset focused on engagement and encouragement.

By nature human beings are highly impressionable. That characteristic is critically important as we develop from infants to children to young adults. We observe the people around us and learn how to navigate the world. At some point, however, our impressionable nature can become problematic. We allow others to describe and rate our abilities and potential – more often than not in ways that are limiting and denigrating. Even worse, we do the same thing to ourselves. It's a truism that people are often their own harshest critics and, as a direct result, their worst enemies. Henry Ford famously observed:

> **"Whether you think you can or think you can't, you're right."**

The corollary to Ford's aphorism is this: "Whether you think they can or think they can't, you'll pave the way for their success or failure." When people believe you have a high opinion of them, they will rise to their level of excellence and your level of expectation. Goethe stated the concept like this: "Treat a man as he appears to be and you make him worse. But treat a man as if he already were what he potentially could be, and you make him what he should be."

As with all character-related issues, the choice is yours. You can create and exude a nurturing mindset that expands horizons for yourself and others; or you can erect constraining walls driven by fear, jealousy, insecurity, and anger. One contributes; the other detracts. There are no shades of gray.

Choose Your Spots

Your personal contribution to someone else's success is most important when times are bad and self-esteem is at its lowest. Kevin McHale, the former Boston Celtics great, once asked his coach K.C. Jones why he always patted someone on the back after they made a poor shot but never congratulated them on a great shot. K.C. said this: "After you've made the winning basket, you've got 15,000 people cheering for you. TV stations come at you, and everybody's giving you high-fives. You don't need me then. When you need a real friend is when you feel that nobody likes you."

K.C. Jones understood that it takes considerably less effort – both physically and emotionally – to recognize success with a pat on the back to someone who's standing tall in victory than what's required to help lift someone off the ground after defeat. But think about McHale's question and Jones' answer. Everyone wants a piece of you (and a vicarious share of the glory) when you're a hero – so many people in fact that they tend to merge into one and are easily forgotten. The flipside is quite different. The person behind the hand that reaches out to lift you up is someone you'll always remember. That act of kindness and support will create a bond that can never be broken. There is of course a different scenario. Rather than lend a helping hand to someone in need, many people choose to ignore the situation, walk away, or give the proverbial kick to a man who's down. Those people will also be remembered but more like sour acid in the gut rather than honeyed warmth in the heart.

Unleash Your Improvisational Yes-Man (or Woman)

No, we are not recommending that you become an ass-kissing sycophant. Instead we urge you to recognize the power of positivity – positive energy, words, emotions, actions, and body language. And we urge you to look to improvisational comedy for validation of an affirmative approach to life.

Improvisational comedy is built upon one hard and fast rule – always agree with whatever your partner inserts into the bit. If A says you're in a tent in the jungles of South America, B can't counter him by saying you're in an igloo just miles from the North Pole. A and B are equally responsible for their success – and thus equally responsible for laying a comedic egg. The secret of successful improvisation is accepting the premise you're presented and building upon it in a way that leads the next performer to another "Yes, and..." adlib. In truth, the best improvisational actors go one step further. They don't just lead their partner to another adlib; they provide an inspirational pathway to comedic genius.

As much as we believe that everyday life can be viewed as a comedy, we know that you can't actually live as though you're an improvisational actor. Or can you? In *Bossy Pants* Tina Fey writes, "in real life you're not always going to agree with everything everyone says. But the Rule of Agreement reminds you to respect what your partner has created and to at least start from an open-minded place. Start with a YES and see where that takes you." Fey goes on to say,

"I always find it jarring when I meet someone in real life whose first answer is no."

Negativity is indeed jarring and far too common in our daily interactions. Negativity cuts off creativity, damages relationships, and blocks collaboration. That's why negativity and judgmental comments of any kind are prohibited in brainstorming sessions. Every idea has some merit (even if buried deep beneath the surface). The seemingly stupidest idea you've ever heard can team up with one or two other mediocre ideas and be transformed into a concept of incredible brilliance. But that can only happen if these stupid and mediocre ideas are not treated as dead-on-arrival. Countless breakthroughs in art and science have undoubtedly been squelched by the negative feedback of nearsighted naysayers. And with equal certainty, those naysayers will not generate breakthrough thinking. Indeed it's unlikely that inveterate nay-sayers do any serious thinking at all.

Let Them Read Your Mind

Inspiration is like love – the word is cheap and meaningless unless backed by genuine emotion. You will never inspire someone to achieve ever-greater heights just by saying the words. The other person has to *feel* your inspirational effect. Your inspirational tendency needs to become innate. It's not something you do; it's part of who you are. Here's how to think about it. Make believe people can read your mind. They know exactly what you're thinking, so when you say "better luck next time" they would know your actual thought is "give it up because this is the best you'll ever be." If this were indeed the case, they would know unequivocally that you're a liar and a fake and whatever relationship you had would be severely damaged. If on the other hand, your voice says "better luck next time" and your innermost thoughts believe "this misstep will serve to make you better and stronger," your credibility and personal connection will be forever enhanced.

Taken together this means we can't supply a list of go-to phrases and tricks of the inspirational trade that can transform you into an effective leader or mentor. Instead we can describe the key attributes of a 20/20 mindset focused on establishing and maintaining strong interpersonal relationships within a context of mutual inspiration.

- *Emotionally open* – All inspiration is emotional and built on a foundation of trust. In order to truly influence others you must first create an emotional connection, and it must be an emotional connection that flows both ways. Many people are reluctant to share emotional bonds because they think it makes them look weak and vulnerable. The truth is quite the opposite. Emotion is a sign of human depth and caring. The robots of the future, no matter how technologically advanced, will never be able to empathize. Empathy is the clearest demonstration that "I've traveled in your shoes" and "truly understand your victories and defeats."

- *Passionately consistent* – Clarence Clemons, the deceased saxophonist for the E-Street Band, said this of Bruce Springsteen: "I believed in him like I believe in God…He was always so straight and dedicated to what he believes, you became a believer simply by being around him." It's hard to inspire others if your behavior contradicts your words.

- *Other-focused* – People will believe in you because you believe in them. Rather than always focusing on what's best for you, devote time and attention to helping others reach their potential. And even more importantly, inspirational leaders actively seek potential in others – and delight when that potential is achieved.

- *Highly visual* – The greatest accomplishments in human history have been driven by dreams. Dreams like Thomas Edison's to light up the world. President Kennedy's to put a man on the moon by the end of the decade. Nelson Mandela's dream to end apartheid in South Africa. These dreams became reality because, when spoken aloud, they painted a vivid picture of what the end-result would look like. That's how great leaders inspire – they *show* rather than simply *tell*. (Check out Simon Sinek's classic TED Talk, "How Great Leaders Inspire Action," for additional insight.)

- *Results-oriented* – Steve Jobs could be a nasty taskmaster but he also inspired people to accomplish what they had previously viewed as the impossible. He didn't play nice to win friends; instead he was brutally honest and earned the respect and gratitude of everyone who surpassed their personal best because of his prompting.

- *Physically aware* – The way you deliver a message provides a clue about your sincerity and a cue about how the recipient should react. Before speaking think about how your posture, vocal intonation, and volume might be perceived by the listener and whether that perception is consistent with your intent. Also consider the location and timing of the situation. Would it be better to have this interaction in private or in a crowded coffee shop? Would the outcome likely be better, and more aligned with your intent, if you delayed the interaction to a later time?

- *Fun-filled* – Negativists take life way too seriously and, because they drag down anyone within their radioactive field, people try to avoid them. Esteem-builders, on the other hand, create an environment of hope and buoyancy that attracts people. They take pleasure in the simple activities of life and are fun to be around. It's not because they tell jokes but rather because they understand life is meant to be enjoyed or it will mean nothing.

- *Empowering-enablers* – As much as we hate how these two words have been co-opted into dismissive business clichés and psycho-babble drivel, their core meanings remain critical in the character make-up of true leaders and respected mentors. Individuals with fully developed 20/20 mindsets *empower* others to think on their own rather than shackling them to one's own beliefs. Further they *enable* others – via the contribution of time, resources, and education – to accomplish their personal goals and achieve their own dreams.

- *Purposeful* – Great leaders possess a long-term vision and they share it openly. They live and work with a purpose. And that purpose almost always boils down to the betterment of the human condition – locally and globally.

> **"It's hard to inspire others if your behavior contradicts your words."**

20/20 Sight Line: See The Good In The Really Bad

In *The Power of Nice*, co-authors Linda Kaplan Thaler and Robin Koval describe an unusual exercise used by couples therapist Dr. Ona Robinson. Couples frequently fall into contrarian mode when interacting with their spouse. To counter that tendency Dr. Robinson asks the couple to work together and provide at least three reasons why cannibalism is good. As

Thaler and Koval write, "She gets a lot of hilarious responses – 'excellent source of protein,' 'not too much fat,' 'reduces world population,' 'all-natural ingredients.'" In the end, the couples begin to realize that you can think and speak positively about anything; and Dr. Robinson hopes that realization will help break negative communication habits and nurture a more enriching relationship.

Your assignment is to use a similar approach and list at least three positive aspects of these decidedly stupid product ideas (which we know some of you will undoubtedly steal and make millions from):

- Pizza in a Cup
- Battery-Powered Espresso Machine
- Shoes With Built-In Metal Detector
- Soft Drink That Gives You a 24-Hour Jersey Tan
- Powdered Water

Please visit us at **20-20MindSight.com/chapter14** to download the worksheet, access new content, see how others have completed the exercise, and maybe share your results.

CHAPTER 15: *"EASY TO MAKE A BUCK"*

Leave Your Mark

As part of a personal assessment paper, Phil asks his senior undergraduate students to write the eulogy they'd like to have spoken at their funerals. These are 21- and 22-year-old students who don't know where they're going to be working or living after graduation and have given zero thought to how they'd like to be remembered 60 or 80 years in the future. Many have said that they were initially "creeped out" by the assignment, but by the end of the semester, they're unanimous in believing it was the most impactful thing they'd ever done. It got them focused on their legacies – how the world and the people around them would be affected by their presence.

Tom Brokaw, the news anchor and best-selling author, said, "It's easy to make a buck. It's a lot tougher to make a difference." The latter, however, is what most of us want to accomplish in our heart of hearts. Nonetheless, very few of us think about how we can make a *profound* difference by truly touching our family, friends, colleagues, neighbors, and communities. Aristotle taught that we help others to be happier by helping them to become better – i.e., to be better for having known you. That is a legacy anyone can be proud of, and the legacy everyone should strive to achieve.

> **"It's easy to make a buck. It's a lot tougher to make a difference."**

Define And Embrace Your Purpose

In his classic *Man's Search for Meaning,* the Holocaust survivor Viktor Frankl stated, "man's main concern is not to gain pleasure or to avoid pain but rather to see a meaning in his life." Frankl's use of the term "meaning" suggests an outward and upward search rather than inward and downward. If we were to compare human beings to corporations for a moment, we can equate "meaning" to "mission." A company's mission statement is intended to articulate why the company exists – the purpose and intent at its core. The meaning of one's life is the same – i.e., the overarching purpose of our lives and how we will demonstrate it in our day-to-day activities.

The purest example of just how powerful this desire to find meaning and make a difference that lasts beyond our mortal lives comes from Steve Jobs. In 1983, Jobs was leading the search for a new leader for Apple Computer (as it was then known). He went hard after John Scully, the President of Pepsi-Cola. After multiple discussions, Jobs asked the question that is now legendary and, at the time, served to close the deal. Jobs asked Scully, "Do you want to sell sugar water for the rest of your life, or do you want to come with me and change the world?" Keep in mind that Scully was already wildly successful. He was president of a world-class company, widely recognized as a marketing genius, and wealthier than any human being needs to be. But in the end he realized he was simply pushing a product and he could not rationally or emotionally walk away from an opportunity to have a real and lasting effect on quite literally billions of people across every continent. That's what made Scully accept the position at Apple. He was already making a good buck, now he could make a significant difference.

We bet all of you would have made the same decision once Jobs spelled out the difference between working at Pepsi versus Apple. What if he hadn't? What if he had simply focused on the opportunity for greater wealth via stock options or the increased prestige of heading up a sexy, high-tech growth company compared to a ho-hum beverage company? Would Scully have accepted? Would you have? And more importantly, have you or are you now ignoring decisions and opportunities that would give greater meaning and fulfillment to your life? Does your job complement or contradict your personal philosophy and goals? Does your personal life within your family and community provide a sense of contribution or are you mindlessly going through the motions? Are you asking the right questions to drive an honest answer? Do you know the right questions?

Does your job complement or contradict your personal philosophy and goals?

It would be impossible to provide a template to help guide you through the process of identifying how best to add value to your life and the people around you, but we believe the question posed by Jobs can help jumpstart the process. Just fill in the blanks:

Do you want to _____ for the rest of your life?

Or do you want to _____

Make Every Opportunity Count

When Phil ran the marketing groups for several large firms, he always stressed that everyone in the company, regardless of title or function, was a marketer. Every employee whether in HR, finance, customer service, sales, or wherever touched the customer in some way and thus contributed to building up or dragging down the firm's brand and reputation. Every customer touch-point – from mobile apps to printed statements to the music that played while customers were on-hold – created an opportunity to enhance or damage perception of the firm. They were opportunities that could not be wasted.

Much of Jillian's career has been focused on building connections between people. In her workshops and presentations Jillian provides real-life examples of how seemingly random, everyday interactions can lead to long-lasting, mutually beneficial relationships. She demonstrates how she's been able to initiate personal connections in virtually any situation – in line at Starbucks, on a bus in Thailand, on a surfing beach in San Diego, and in crowded hotel conference rooms full of old white men who would seem to have nothing in common with a vivacious young woman. Whatever the situation, Jillian is proactive in initiating the contact and she works hard to make the relationship deeper and stronger over time.

The approaches that Jillian and Phil describe may seem different on the surface, but they're actually quite similar. Every new day delivers multiple opportunities to make a difference. Part of that opportunity centers on the importance of making a good first impression but that's the easy part. We all know charming glad-handers with big smiles and pearly whites. They're all about quantity rather than quality. They're like stereotypical politicians who believe if you shake enough hands and kiss enough babies someone is bound to remember you. The truth is that some people will indeed remember the glad-hander, but the glad-hander will remember no one. The glad-hander is looking to get something – a vote, promotion, donation, or some other type of recognition. One's true intent when meeting someone is usually revealed within a few moments. People can tell when your interest is genuine or phony by *how you make them feel*. Genuine interest engenders positive feelings and those feelings are what people remember.

The kind of first impression we advocate opens the door to a memorable interaction for both parties. It's an impression that is notable not for forced smiles but for genuine interest and relevance. It presents a shared opportunity to identify common interests and concerns. It is never designed to "close a deal." Its sole purpose is to create a connection that can grow into a relationship that can deepen and broaden over time. The only way to make a difference in someone's life is to first make a connection with them. The more connections, the more opportunities to leave your mark.

> **"People can tell when your interest is genuine or phony by how you make them feel."**

Make Your Choice

We all have the opportunity to choose our life's purpose and direct our energy to making a difference. But that's not the only key decision we make on a daily basis that affects our ability to leave a positive mark on the world. With every action and word we make a decision to:

- Deliver positive or negative energy
- Tell the truth or lie/mislead (even by omission or indifference)
- Inspire or demean
- Be open to new ideas or shut them down
- Give generously or take greedily
- Serve as a role model or a foreboding

- Speak up or remain silent
- Lead or follow

Put The Shoe On The Other Foot

Thus far this chapter has focused on the joy and personal satisfaction that derive from positively impacting another person's life; but there's an equally important flip side to the story – i.e., recognizing and thanking the people who have affected your life. We can all look back and name numerous people that helped guide our way and shape the person we have become. They might be friends, relatives, teachers, coaches, managers, teammates, or colleagues. They might have served as mentor, confidant, sounding board, cheerleader, or even a friendly shoulder to cry on. The point is that they helped you see the big picture, identify your unique skill set and passion, and narrow your focus on the things you held most important. You wouldn't be who you are without their advice and counsel. You know that unequivocally in your heart and mind – but ask yourself this simple question: *Do they know it?*

Have you ever *explicitly* expressed your appreciation for their generous contribution of time and wisdom? Face to face? In writing? In public? Have you told them *exactly* what they did or said that lives with you to this day?

We've purposely highlighted "explicitly" and "exactly" because you need to be precise in your gratitude. A generic "thank you" is grossly insufficient for life-altering insights and revelations. It's important that your expression of thanks has a profound effect on the recipient. Learning how much they contributed to your life will help your benefactors realize their own goal of living an impactful life – and encourage them to help others in the same way.

Perhaps the most powerful expression of appreciation is the promise to use their generosity as the framework for your own life. Promise to pay it forward just as they did – with no quid pro quo expectations but rather just the desire to help another human being navigate this sometimes perilous and confusing world.

And Don't Forget The Other's Other Foot

As inherently good as we believe most people to be, we all take occasional missteps and tumble into a chasm of selfishness, vulgarity, churlishness, and otherwise mean-spirited asshole behavior. It doesn't mean we're assholes – unless, of course, we fail to make amends.

"I'm sorry" are the two most difficult words for many people to say aloud. They represent an acknowledgment that we were wrong for something we said or did. We almost always know when we hurt someone – whether purposely or accidentally – and in a perfect world, we would always be willing to accept responsibility and apologize. The Catch 22, however, is that virtually nothing is ever 100% one person's fault. Both parties usually play a part in creating and escalating the situation that prompted the wrongdoing, and it is precisely this dual responsibility that stops us from apologizing as often as we should. To wit:

Why should I apologize? She started it.
I'll apologize if he does.
She'll never apologize, but if she does she won't mean it.
Why am I always the one who apologizes?

A heartfelt apology is magnanimity in the fullest definition of the word. Apologies should be offered generously and forgivingly. Sure both parties might have been at fault and the other party may not yet or may never acknowledge their role, but that's okay. Your acceptance of responsibility and expression of regret is all that really matters. We can only be responsible for our own behavior. Waiting for the other person to apologize first demonstrates a type of co-dependency that is never in anyone's best interests. By apologizing you will have done the right thing and, in the spirit of stranger things have happened, your apology may eventually prompt the recalcitrant to follow your lead and acknowledge their own mistakes and transgressions to you or to others in the future. That's another way to pay it forward and make a difference.

20/20 Sight Line: Questions To Ask Yourself

There is no single way to ensure that you make a difference. Much of it depends on our unique circumstances. Nonetheless we can offer a list of questions which, if answered truthfully, can help guide you to a purposeful life with long-lasting impact and influences.

For each question, give yourself a 3 for every "Yes" answer, a 2 for "Sometimes" and a 1 for "Never."

Yes – 3   Sometimes – 2   Never – 1

- When I lay my head on the pillow at night can I identify at least one person that benefited by interacting with me? _____

- Do I ask questions that elicit thoughtful responses? _____

- Do I do or say things that would horrify me if reported on the front page of *The New York Times*? _____

- Am I more focused on *being* good than *doing* good? _____

- Do I recognize my personal strengths and weaknesses (and have a game plan to leverage the former and improve the latter)? _____

- Do I regularly recognize and praise others' core character traits and values? _____

- Do my conversations revolve around me and my needs versus the interests and concerns of others?

- Do I learn something every day? _____

- Do I teach something every day? _____

- Do I meet someone new every day? _____

Total Score: _____

Please visit us at **20-20MindSight.com/chapter15** to access the worksheet and see what your score means.

The great Jackie Robinson who broke the color barrier in major league baseball and positively affected millions of people around the world said, "A life is not important except in the impact it has on other lives." As you consider the questions listed above think about Robinson's words and, going back to Tom Brokaw's quote, ask yourself at the end of every day whether you just made a buck or did you truly make a difference?

> *"A life is not important except in the impact it has on other lives."*

CHAPTER 16: *"SOMEONE WHO CAN'T REPAY YOU"*

Join Hands

t's ironic but an argument can be made that the more "connected" we become via today's all-pervasive social media the less connected and more isolated we feel. No quantity of Facebook updates and Tweets – and their emphasis on *I*, *me*, and *mine* – can compare to a single face-to-face, *we*-focused conversation. It's equally ironic that our culture promotes a zero-sum mentality where I win if you lose and individual achievement trumps teamwork and collaboration. It's all about *Us* versus *Them*, but that's not how life really works. Very few situations truly pit one individual against another. The vast majority of the time *We* all benefit by working together and placing the group above the individual.

Today, the concepts of connectedness and relationship-building have been replaced by a focus on transactional networking. Indeed, most authors in the leadership, success, and personal branding space emphasize the need to expand and leverage our professional networks. Much of their advice, however, focuses on a quid pro quo mindset: "If I do this for them, then they'll do that for me." In light of that nonsensical attitude, the words of seventeenth-century writer John Bunyan are especially relevant in today's networking-obsessed world: "You have not lived today until you have done something for someone who can never repay you." Networking is not about manipulative schmoozing designed to help you get a new job or achieve some other short-term goal. Rather it's about building mutually beneficial bonds (based on common interests) with no expectation that a service you provide will be reciprocated in the future.

Stop Networking And Start Relating

Jillian has been a frequent guest lecturer in Phil's Communications & Personal Branding course at Boston College. She speaks about her area of expertise, networking; and she always receives high marks from the students. Here's what one student wrote:

> I'd always thought of networking as a tool. Anytime I heard some-one mention the importance of networking it was used as a means to an end. That end was job-hunting, business-boosting, or some other self-serving activity. As a result, this idea of staying in touch to build a network seemed more than a little insincere. My thinking was that since I had spent such a small amount of time with them (often just a few minutes), they would surely be suspicious if I contacted them to follow up our conversation.
>
> After listening to Jillian, however, I've begun to view networking as being similar to having a garden. Nothing grows overnight and noth-ing is ready to be harvested for months after planting the seed. Jillian taught me that a network is not a mailing list – it's a community. Her stories about contacting people in her network to grab a coffee or just touch base made me realize that effective networking is geared towards genuine human interaction and concern rather than just de-layed self-interest.

Networking must never be viewed as a transaction. It's a journey rather than an end. Most importantly, networking is not a numbers game where more is better. The depth and quality of your connections is of utmost im-portance. You are indeed known by the company you keep, so focus on building quality relationships with quality people.

Are You A Pencil Point Or Intestinal Villi?

The first step in connecting with people on an honest and genuine authentic basis is to be genuine from the very start. Unfortunately that's where most people make their critical mistake. When presented with networking opportunities, people tend to position themselves one-dimensionally.

If these one-dimensional networkers were pencils they would show off their tips – the graphite point where the work of a pencil gets done – and only the tip. Stop reading for a moment and see what we mean. Pick up a pen or pencil as if you're going to write with it. However, instead of placing the tip on paper, rotate the pencil so you're staring into the point head-on. From this viewpoint, the instrument appears to be flatly one-dimensional and devoid of any visual appeal. Indeed, from this perspective, it would be difficult to distinguish a Bic pen point from a Mont Blanc. That is precisely the problem with presenting yourself as a narrowly focused, one-trick pony. If you feature your pencil point as a door-opener, you will end up gone and forgotten – smudged and erased – long before your business card is tossed in the trash.

So pencils are clearly better than pencil points, but you know what's even better at initiating and maintaining personal relationships? Intestinal villi. You read it right. Instead of randomly working a room, trying to poke people with your pencil point like a crazed woodpecker, imagine yourself as the undulating finger-like projections of intestinal villi whose sole focus is on absorbing nutrients. The multi-dimensional structure of villi significantly increases the overall surface area, thereby creating maximum opportunity for absorption. Effective networkers do the same thing. Instead of absorbing nutrients, they focus on exponentially increasing opportunities to create connections that can be strengthened and nurtured over time. Rather than trumpeting their one "special talent" (which is certainly shared by countless others, many of whom are probably in the same room and showing off the same razor-sharp pencil point), effective networkers highlight their multi-faceted character traits. That approach elicits an emotional response and a deeper connection which allows them to discover the issues that matter most to the other person, which prompts a more relevant conversation, which in turn makes them stand out in an increasingly crowded world.

Practice *Ubuntu*
The South African term *Ubuntu* was introduced in the mid-nineteenth century and popularized throughout the world in the late-twentieth century by Archbishop Desmond Tutu and Nelson Mandela. There is no precise

translation of *Ubuntu* into English, but its meaning is usually distilled down to the concept of a universal bond that unites all of humanity. In 2008 Archbishop Tutu explained *Ubuntu* as "the essence of being human" with these words:

> *Ubuntu speaks particularly about the fact that you can't exist as a human being in isolation. It speaks about our interconnectedness. You can't be human all by yourself; and when you have this quality – Ubuntu – you are known for your generosity.*
>
> *We think of ourselves far too frequently as just individuals separated from one another, whereas you are connected and what you do affects the whole world. When you do well, it spreads out; it is for the whole of humanity.*

Nelson Mandela expanded upon this description with one caveat: "*Ubuntu* does not mean that people should not enrich themselves." Instead he posed the question we all must answer in our daily activities and interactions: "Are you going to do so in order to enable the community around you to be able to improve?"

Embracing *Ubuntu* is the most direct route to a 20/20 mindset focused on building a community of like-minded people. Archbishop Tutu has said we all "belong in the bundle of life." If you replace the concept of "building a network" with "building a bundle of life," you'll take a huge step toward.

Desperate Is As Desperate Does

The best-selling author Keith Ferrazzi, who has been described by *Forbes* magazine as one of the world's most connected individuals, provides a crisp and powerful summary of what networking is and isn't. He says when people ask for advice on how to build a network to find a job *now*, he tells them to forget it. Why? Because "People can tell the difference between desperation and an earnest attempt to create a relationship."

No one wants to be viewed as desperate, yet we all know people who contact us out of the blue and then invite us to "network over coffee or lunch." There may have been zero interaction between the two of you for years, and the interaction way back when may have been unmemorable at best. You know – and they usually do as well – that they're hitting rock bottom, time is running out and they're throwing a wobbly Hail Mary pass.

Don't let that ever happen to you. Everyone will need assistance from others at some point in their professional lives, and that's okay. But don't let yourself be known as a desperate "taker" who is only interested in others when it's to your benefit. Instead be a generous "giver" of time and counsel. Make it a habit to reach out to people just to say hello, check-in, or acknowledge something they're doing. Those "just because" communications are interpersonal gifts that will repay you multiple times in multiple ways.

It's easy and it's fun.

> **"People can tell the difference between desperation and an earnest attempt to create a relationship."**

Connect To Collaborate

It's hard to argue against the fact that the best work in any field is achieved through collaboration. History includes few examples of people who succeeded entirely on their own. We often attribute success to specific individuals and their unique genius and skill set, but the reality usually tells a different story. Michael Jordan benefitted by playing alongside Scottie Pippen. Steve Jobs' original vision was executed by Steve Wozniak. And Walt Disney had a team of animators and writers to bring his ideas to life. None of this detracts from the extraordinary accomplishments of these individuals, but it's fair to suggest that Steve Jobs would not have risen to international acclaim if he'd had to build and program the first Apple computer on his own.

Collaboration came naturally to our ancestors. They organized themselves into small groups – hunting teams, tribes, communities, city-states, etc. – for the benefit of all. This cooperative mindset was a huge factor in early humans' ability to brave the harshest of elements and disperse to Earth's furthest frontiers.

Collaboration doesn't come quite so easy or naturally today. Our world celebrates individual achievement and personal advancement. We all want our fifteen minutes of fame, but we'd rather not share the spotlight.

Collaboration requires a commitment – a commitment to a shared goal. A commitment that fully understands we might end up playing the role of Scottie Pippen or the little-known Disney animator, Ubbe Iwerks, who designed the iconic Mickey Mouse. We don't presume to know the inner workings of Pippen or Iwerks, but we doubt either is terribly upset with the results of their behind-the-scenes status. Pippen won six NBA championships playing in Jordan's shadow and Iwerks received two Academy Awards among other honors for his collaborations with Walt Disney.

The moral is that collaboration doesn't mean each collaborator can't achieve his or her own personal best. In fact the opposite is often true. When you collaborate with someone whose skills are different or superior to your own, you'll get better. Plus you'll significantly improve the chances of realizing your own dreams.

20/20 Sight Line: "The Collaborative Way"

Most people believe – or assume – they are good collaborators. There is no quantitative way to measure collaborative effectiveness; but Lloyd Fickett & Associates, a consulting firm focused on helping organizations improve employee leadership and collaboration, offers a self-assessment survey that is the best tool we've come across. We urge you to complete the survey available as a download at **20-20MindSight.com/chapter16**.

The Collaborative Way® Survey

Date of self-assesment ___ / ___ / _____

Please rate your own practice level on each dimension below from 1 (Worst Level) to 10 (Best Level) based on your view of your conversations, actions, and contributions over the past 2–3 months. Please be honest with yourself, rating yourself as if you were observing yourself, without being overly critical and without sugar-coating. There is no neutral value, with 5 being slightly below your expectations and six being slightly above your expectations.

Listening Generously   1= Worst Level   1 2 3 4 5 6 7 8 9 10   10= Best

With Curiosity and an Intention to Learn:	Not really interested in other points of view or what others have to say. Interrupts and forces opinions on others.		Genuinely interested in why people say what they say. Asks questions to gain further knowledge and understanding.
Willing to be Influenced:	Doesn't want to change, compromise or accept other opinions. Uses listening only to find a way to make a point.		Open to new ideas, trying new things, and revising opinions. Listens with an openness to modifying a personal point of view.
Setting Aside Filters:	Judges what people say based on past experiences and pre-conceived ideas.		Listens objectively without assumptions about what people will say or do. Sets aside preconceived perspectives and conclusions.
Replicating and Recreating:	Rarely strives to listen beyond what is being said. Unable to re-state what the other person said.		For clarity, re-states what the other person has said. Reflects an appreciation of where the other person is coming from, including commitments and feelings.
Influencing Action:	Is quick to give advice and rarely strives to understand the other person's situation.		Before giving advice, recommendations or other input, first attempts to appreciate the other person's perspective.
Average for Listening Generously:			

Access to *The Collaborative Way Survey* is provided as a courtesy and with the permission of the copyright owner: Lloyd Fickett & Associates. Learn more at http://collaborativeway.com

CHAPTER 17: *"THE SECRET OF EVERYTHING"*

Keep It Together

Athletes call it "being in the zone" when every part of their game fits together and they're performing at the peak of their ability. Individuals in every aspect of their lives can experience that same level of in-the-zone achievement via the power of integrative thinking. The trick is to take a broader view of the world and the issues that face us in our daily lives. All of our thoughts, actions, and beliefs reside on a Mobius loop (a spiral-like continuous circle) rather than the extremes of a straight-line continuum. Swami Vivekananda poetically summarized the concept of a truly integrated mindset like this:

"All differences in this world are of degree, and not of a kind, because oneness is the secret of everything."

Go Analog

Computers exist in a binary world; humans do not. Nonetheless most people seem to operate as though constrained by on-off decision-making. They evaluate situations, weigh alternatives, and consider issues within a yes-no, either-or, black-white framework. The result is a "binary mindset" that excludes the maybes, both-ands, and thousand shades of gray that exemplify and greatly enrich life.

The solution – as with many things in life – is to take a step back. In this particular example we'd encourage you to embrace a more nuanced "analog" way of thinking. Borrowing from the scientific definition of analog – "information represented by a continuously variable physical quantity" – analog thinking represents the ability and the willingness to change one's mind based on new information. Ironically this analog mindset can be viewed as a negative. Politicians are frequently labeled flip-floppers for changing their view on an issue. The alternative, however, is to hold hard and fast to one's opinion despite new evidence to the contrary – a mindset that few would proudly admit to embracing.

F. Scott Fitzgerald observed that the true test of intelligence was "the ability to hold two opposing ideas in mind at the same time and still retain the ability to function. One should, for example, be able to see that things are hopeless yet be determined to make them otherwise." Walt Whitman took the idea one step further with these lines: "Do I contradict myself? Very well then. I contradict myself. I am large. I contain multitudes." Fitzgerald and Whitman point to the fact that seemingly contradictory beliefs and ideas can be brought together in a synthesis that is far superior to either of the conflicting ideas.

Synthesize For Fun And Profit

The dictionary defines *synthesis* as "the combination of ideas to form a theory or system" and "the final stage in the process of dialectical reasoning, in which a new idea resolves the conflict between thesis and antithesis." *Synergy* is the close cousin of synthesis and is defined as "the interaction or cooperation of two or more organizations, substances, or other agents to produce a combined effect greater than the sum of their separate effects."

One need look no further than the natural world to see the powerful effects of synergy. Bees feed off the nectar of flowering plants and thereby support the propagation of those plants via pollination. Intestinal bacteria help many species – including our own – break down and digest food. And the big cats of Africa will work together to hunt and bring down large prey like Cape buffalo and giraffes.

Within the human mind, the ability to synthesize – via big-picture, analog thinking – helps people use their broad vision and integrative mindset to see what others miss. Synthesis provides context and identifies A+B synergies that can maximize results. Binary thinking delivers familiar answers that are quantitative, pre-tested, and pre-approved. Synthesizing can deliver innovation, new ideas, and brilliantly efficient solutions that seem so simple in retrospect it's a wonder no one thought of them sooner.

Except it's not a wonder at all.

Twenty-first century Americans are not taught how to develop an integrative mindset. Nor do they appreciate the power and inherent value of analog thinking. To the contrary, our society often discourages – and sometimes disciplines – young minds that pursue larger truths, that ask questions no one wants to hear, that look to the future rather than the past.

Binary thinking supports indoctrination, groupthink, and stubborn adherence to *the way things have always been*. A+B always equals C. Analog thinking – for the very reason that it goes deeper and continually seeks new inputs – delivers the profound insight that there is no "way things have always been." Change is a constant. Nothing is exactly as it was yesterday, last year, or a century ago. A+B might still equal C, but it's just as likely to equal ABC, or D-E, or maybe even XYZ.

When the binary, non-synthesized mind waxes poetic about the "way things have always been," it's really pointing to a particular point in time. *This* is how it was in 1955, in the nineteenth century, in colonial times or in the generalized "old days." It's a desire to have things be as they were at whatever time you choose to posit as the ideal. The synthesized mind understands that your idealized point in time will be different from mine which will be different from everyone else's – perhaps by a wide margin or maybe just the slightest of degrees.

There is only one *real* world, yet everyone perceives and experiences it differently. That means we each possess our own "reality." Within a binary mindset, either my reality is right and yours is wrong or vice-versa. A 20/20 mindset that embraces the broad vision and uniting power of synthesis accepts and allows for the other person's reality. Why is that? Because the other person's reality is a component of the "real" world we experience – a component just as important as our own reality.

That ability – using analog thinking and synergy in the broadest sense of the terms – to simultaneously see and understand our own reality, every other person's reality, and the "real reality" is what we would humbly refer to as the Platonic ideal of *20/20 Mind Sight*.

Realize and Accept

In 1943, Abraham Maslow introduced the psychology of human potential to a broad audience via his "hierarchy of needs" pyramid. Seventy-plus years later it is still taught in high schools and colleges despite widespread criticism of Maslow's data-collection processes, suspect assumptions, and highly subjective interpretations.

We've never been fans of Maslow's hierarchy of needs. Its sequential, step-by-step approach to personal motivation, growth, and achievement is overly simplistic. Life is anything but linear, and humans are faced with a multitude of necessities, motivations, and goals that go far beyond what Maslow outlined. Our biggest issue with Maslow is that, although he sometimes characterized self-actualization as a birthright, he seemed to hold the mass of people in rather low regard. In *Towards a Psychology of Being*, Maslow stated, "Though, in principle, self-actualization is easy, in practice it rarely happens (by my criteria, certainly in less than 1% of the adult population)." Maslow counted Albert Einstein and Henry David Thoreau among the lofty ranks of the self-actualized and used their ilk as the benchmark for self-actualization. That is akin to suggesting that Ken Griffey Jr. was not a baseball superstar because he failed to match Babe Ruth's achievements.

Notwithstanding these issues regarding his hierarchy of needs, Maslow's depiction of the "peak experience" aspect of self-actualization is highly relevant to the 20/20 mindset. Going back to that over-used sports metaphor, Maslow described peak experience in a way that is virtually identical to what athletes refer to as "being in the zone." It was experiencing life as it was meant to be experienced. Things *were* as they *ought to be*. Specifically, from *Towards a Psychology of Being*:

> *The person in the peak-experiences usually feels himself to be at the peak of his powers, using all his capacities at the best and fullest... He feels more intelligent, more perceptive, wittier, stronger, or more graceful than at other times...He is no longer wasting effort fighting and restraining himself; muscles are no longer fighting muscles. In the normal situation, part of our capacities are used for action, and part are wasted on restraining these same capacities. Now there is no waste...He becomes like a river without dams.*

Maslow's peak experience constitutes the profound *realization* of one's inner character. From our perspective, realization has multiple meanings and ramifications. At the foundational level, it means converting one's potential into reality. More importantly, it relates to the vivid capture and strong embrace of this reality by the mind's eye. Realization and self-acceptance allow us to acknowledge our strengths and weaknesses. It allows us to celebrate our independence without ignoring our various dependencies and interdependencies. And it ensures that we never allow our lives to be driven solely by external factors.

This realization of one's character is not an abstract, subconscious process. The fully realized individual recognizes, understands, and deeply appreciates his or her achievement. It's an earned achievement that does not come without hard work and focused effort. It's an achievement that deserves to be celebrated.

One way to think about this is to consider the difference between *knowing* something and *realizing* it. In this dichotomy, knowledge represents more of a surface-level accumulation of facts and figures. Realization, on the other hand, comprises an inner acceptance of a deeply felt wisdom. Realization goes far beyond understanding. Realization is a fully engaged, visceral acceptance of a newly discovered internal or external truth.

Realization brings with it an inner calm. It delivers a state of uncomplicated innocence and guilelessness. There are no woulda-coulda-shoulda doubts. Preoccupation with the past or the future is replaced with an intense focus on the present. There's a unification of mind, body, and soul; and there's a discovery of the perfect balance between selfishness and selflessness. Because it is indeed a perfect balance, the hard work must continue throughout our lives. The fully realized, insightful mindset requires diligent monitoring.

Maslow referred to self-actualization as the "fusion of the person with the world." We live in a world that is changing at an ever-increasing pace. The communities and people around us are continually evolving and the globe is shrinking. Nothing is static and, if we are truly to become and remain one with the world, we need to possess a fluid and dynamic mindset. Without a doubt, we need to be consistent and genuine; but if we stop growing we will fail miserably at our one true goal – living a life of meaning and fulfillment.

"Realization goes far beyond understanding."

20/20 Sight Line: Are You Satisfied?

The "Satisfaction With Life Scale" was developed and introduced to the world by Ed Diener, Robert A. Emmons, Randy J. Larsen, and Sharon Griffin in 1985. The scale uses a 5-item survey to assess general satisfaction with the respondent's life as a whole. It is not designed to measure satisfaction with specific areas of one's life such as health or finances.

The worksheet, scoring grid, and explanation of your score are available at: **20-20MindSight.com/chapter17**

The Satisfaction with Life Scale

DIRECTIONS: Below are five statements with which you may agree or disagree. Using the 1-7 scale below, indicate your agreement with each item by placing the appropriate number in the line preceding that item. Please be open and honest in your responding.

1 = Strongly Disagree
2 = Disagree
3 = Slightly Disagree
4 =Neither Agree or Disagree
5 = Slightly Agree
6 = Agree
7 = Strongly Agree

____ 1. In most ways my life is close to ideal.

____ 2. The conditions of my life are excellent.

____ 3. I am satisfied with life.

____ 4. So far I have gotten the important things I want in life.

____ 5. If I could live my life over, I would change almost nothing.

CHAPTER 18: *"THE FEAR OF BEING SIMPLE"*

Cut It To The Core

On July 4, 2012, at an international conference in Geneva, scientists announced the discovery of the Higgs boson – aka the "God particle" – a much-discussed and long sought after fundamental element theorized as being the "spark" that created the universe from "nothingness." Without getting into the hard science of this discovery or its theological implications, the Higgs boson proves the existence of the Higgs field, an invisible force field that permeates the universe. Unlike other force fields like gravity or electromagnetism, the Higgs field does not push or pull other elements – it merely *points*. In a sense it points the way for other elementary particles like quarks and electrons to interact most effectively and efficiently.

The Higgs boson discovery also delivers what can be viewed as the culmination of the reductionist approach to scientific and philosophical inquiry. The ancient Greeks began the process of trying to solve problems by breaking them down to their simplest components. Over the last century scientists have utilized reductionist techniques to continually leapfrog each other and deliver awe-inspiring breakthroughs in molecular biology, quantum physics, and nuclear chemistry.

So what's the relevancy of the Higgs boson to a 20/20 worldview? It's twofold. First, just as the Higgs field points the way for elementary particles, we all possess internal force fields that help guide our various character traits, life experiences, and genetic wiring to work together in powerful harmony. For many of us, this internal force field is similarly invisible and waiting to be discovered and leveraged. And second, reductionism is an invaluable approach to identifying and articulating your core character traits, personal values, and life's mission. By breaking down your personal brand/mission/values to their core components, you're forced to focus. You're forced to make real choices – what to keep and what to eliminate. And, moving from the world of science to art, you're forced to emulate Michelangelo.

"We all possess internal force fields that help guide our various character traits, life experiences, and genetic wiring to work together in powerful harmony."

Unleash Your Inner David

A few years ago, on a family trip to Italy, Phil found himself mesmerized by Michelangelo's *David*. It was far and away the most spectacular piece of artwork he'd ever experienced. The beauty and majesty of the sculpture defy description, and only the most stoic of viewers could not be left breathless. What's particularly fascinating about *David* is that the marble used by Michelangelo had been discarded and long-ignored. The massive block of marble was considered too tall, too narrow, and of an inferior quality. It had been offered to and worked on by several sculptors prior to Michelangelo, but all had walked away from the stone.

Michelangelo, on the other hand, jumped at the opportunity to work on a project of such impressive scale and skill-testing challenges. One could argue that it was his youthful bravado and inexperience that led him to accept a task which others – older and wiser – had summarily rejected. We would argue, instead, that it was due to Michelangelo's ability to visualize the treasure that lay inside the flawed marble. Indeed, Michelangelo believed and stated repeatedly that he did not "sculpt" *David*. Rather, Michelangelo explained that *David* had always existed within the marble. He had simply removed everything that wasn't *David*.

That is precisely what we all need to do when crafting, articulating, and living our own personal brands. Get rid of all the extraneous filler that detracts from one's core character. Get real by getting simple and getting to the core message.

"Get real by getting simple."

It's Not Easy Being Simple

Most people associate complexity with intelligence, but they've got it all wrong. Jack Welch stated it perfectly in a *Harvard Business Review* article: "Insecure managers create complexity. Frightened, nervous managers use thick, convoluted planning books and busy slides filled with everything they've known since childhood. Real leaders don't need clutter. People must have the self-confidence to be clear, precise...You can't believe how hard it is for people to be simple, how much they fear being simple. They worry that if they're simple, people will think they're simple-minded. In reality, of course, it's just the reverse. Clear, tough-minded people are the most simple."

The English language includes 500,000 words. The average American recognizes and understands about 35,000 words but uses less than 3,000 on a regular basis. The exception, of course, is when people are trying to impress others with their erudition, sagacity, and learned modus operandi. That's when the big words and convoluted sentence structure get dusted off and make their grand entrance. Ironically, this type of foppish sophistry accomplishes the de facto goal of making the speaker feel good about himself but fails miserably in communicating and connecting with the intended audience. Obtuseness is a solipsistic obfuscation, and one that is assiduously avoided by effective communicators.

When Phil Knight founded Nike, his battle cry was to "Crush Adidas." Whenever Steve Jobs introduced a new Apple product or service, his overriding goal was to "Change the world." And Walt Disney was determined "to build a magical park" when he envisioned the original Disneyland in California. Each of these statements uses simple words that the average fifth-grader could understand. That means everyone who worked for Nike, Apple, or Disney understood exactly what he or she was working to accomplish. These kinds of statements are simple but also adhere to the tough-minded, cut-it-to-the-core approach that "Neutron Jack" Welch espoused. They helped the Nike, Apple, and Disney teams to follow Michelangelo's example and eliminate every activity that didn't support the overarching goal. They were able to say no to distractions and stay focused on the one and only priority.

Subtract To Add Value And Meaning

In *The Laws of Simplicity* John Maeda states, "Simplicity is about subtracting the obvious and adding the meaningful." That's why creating a simple yet meaningful personal brand is so difficult for many people. Our natural inclination is to cling to the obvious. It's what we know and it feels safe and secure. Subtracting the obvious entails a risk, but with risk – at least well-considered risk – comes reward. If Knight, Jobs, and Disney had avoided risk and stuck with the obvious, none of their innovative products and services would have enriched the world and, in turn, encouraged additional innovation.

> ### *"Simplicity is about subtracting the obvious and adding the meaningful."*

The Japanese have a word – *shibumi* – that refers to elegant simplicity and quiet perfection. It is a state that is highly prized and respected; and it is visible in many aspects of the Japanese culture from the modest décor of Japanese homes, to the peaceful landscapes of zen gardens, to the graceful lines of Japanese calligraphy, and even to the muted power of the traditional martial arts.

What John Maeda and *shibumi* share is an overriding appreciation for the lasting impact of that which is left out or removed. There's a classic book of Chinese verse, *Tao Te Ching*, written around 600 B.C. by the Taoist philosopher, Lao Tzu. The eleventh "chapter" speaks directly to the value of subtraction:

> *Thirty spokes share the wheel's hub;*
> *It is the center hole that makes it useful.*
> *Shape clay into a vessel;*
> *It is the space within that makes it useful.*
> *Cut doors and windows for a room;*
> *It is the holes which make it useful.*
> *Therefore benefit comes from what is there;*
> *Usefulness from what is not there.*

Many Westerners would struggle with the concept that usefulness derives from what is not there. We're used to making things "better" by adding on new features, functions, and whiz-bang gadgetry. We focus on what's there and ignore what isn't. As we go about our daily lives, we focus on what we're doing and hardly question why we're doing it or what we could be doing instead.

This need to fill every available space also extends to most people's communication styles. As a culture, we Americans seem to detest silence and feel compelled to fill every momentary pause in conversation with whatever thought pops into our heads. The next time you're having a one-on-one conversation in person or on the phone try to refrain from talking as soon as the other person finishes a statement. Take some time to think about what you're going to say and how it fits into the flow of the dialogue. We guarantee that your silence – even if only for a couple of seconds – will generate a question like "are you still there?" if you're on the phone or "is everything okay?" if you're face-to-face. Silence, just like white space in design, is a powerful communicator; but just as amateur graphic designers try to fill the page with every possible combination of fonts and colors, most oral communications consist of jousting to see who can cram the greatest number of words into the shortest amount of time.

The adage tells us that less is more; and with the practice of *shibumi*, less will be infinitely more.

> **"Silence, just like white space in design,**
> **is a powerful communicator."**

More Than One Is None

We all do too much, want too much, and have too much. As a result we often value quantity over quality. We experience that phenomenon every day in every aspect of our lives. Consider the never-ending array of new and improved brand extensions that turn simple purchase decisions into mind-numbing calculations of feature-benefit comparisons. Take a walk down the cracker aisle of your local supermarket. The venerable Triscuit cracker, made by Kraft Foods, is now available in ten different varieties: original, reduced fat, cheddar, cracked pepper & olive oil, fire roasted tomato & olive oil, garden herb, deli-style rye, roasted garlic, thin crisps, and rosemary & olive oil. Has anyone's life been bettered by this – including the Kraft corporate coffers (try saying that five times fast)? More choice does not add value. Simple is better than complex. More than one is often none.

The computer is arguably the most complex machine ever invented, yet it is also the most simple. Everything a computer does is in response to switches that are either on or off. Up or down. Who would have ever guessed that all the world's knowledge could be reduced to a series of binary yes-or-no equations? Yet that's exactly what computers do. Everything from *Hamlet* to the theory of relativity can be distilled down to a binary system consisting of no more than Yea or Nay decision-making. The same should be true of your personal brand.

Computers don't make compromises. They are never partly "0" and partly "1". They are unequivocal and focused. They don't strive to be or pretend to be more than they are. All of that is what makes computers so valuable, but it also explains why computers will never (*never say never?*) replace the human brain. The human psyche is anything but unequivocal. We see nuances everywhere and we actively seek compromise. But this interpretive approach to the world usually leads to a lack of focus driven by well-meaning but detrimental concessions and conciliations. We have a natural tendency to want to be all things to all people. We want to be like Swiss army knives, forgetting that the human equivalents of that functional tool are usually viewed as poseurs, flip-floppers, and charlatans who don't believe in or stand for anything.

The antidote is to be focused but not inflexible. Identify what is most important and most meaningful in your life. That's the core of your brand. The first step is identifying it; the second is articulating it. Most of this book has been focused on the former. And rightfully so. Understanding, accepting and embracing your core character is of utmost importance; but it could all be for naught if you can't articulate it simply and concisely.

Simple And Concise

Long before sound bites became synonymous with political campaigns and the reduction of complex sociopolitical issues to pithy ten-second quotations, humans amassed a wide array of short sayings that delivered insight and understanding in a powerful and memorable phrase. Sometimes called proverbs, maxims, aphorisms, or adages, they all shared the structure described by Cervantes as "a short sentence based on long experience." Consider these examples:

- *"Time is money."* Benjamin Franklin
- *"Shared joy is double joy. Shared sorrow is half sorrow."* Swedish Proverb
- *"Real friendship is shown in times of trouble; prosperity is full of friends."* Ralph Waldo Emerson
- *"We make a living by what we get, but we make a life by what we give."* Winston Churchill
- *"Learn as if you were going to live forever. Live as if you were going to die tomorrow."* Mahatma Gandhi

While addressing different aspects of the human condition, each of these statements uses simple language, parallel structure, and a poetic cadence to deliver timeless meaning in a compact package.

Even without the lyrical power of a proverb, each of us has the ability and need to express our personal brand simply and concisely. Here's an example from Bruce Springsteen as quoted in the July 30, 2012 issue of *The New Yorker*: "Once people have bought [their] tickets...that ticket is my handshake. That ticket is me promising you that it's gonna be all the way every chance I get. That's my contract." Springsteen's defining characteristic from his earliest days in Asbury Park has been to sing his heart and lungs out every time he takes the stage. The length of his concerts is legendary, and every audience member feels that Bruce is reading their minds and singing directly to them. Springsteen categorizes his need to connect on a visceral level with his audience as a "contract." We view it as his brand.

Six-Words. No More, No Less.

Abraham Lincoln was arguably America's most insightful and self-reflective president. He was a huge proponent of putting words on paper to help refine his thought processes and ensure that he had adequately and accurately assessed the matter at hand. Your assignment is to channel your inner Lincoln and get to the core of your character by crafting a crisp and concise personal branding statement that eliminates every nonessential and irrelevant component. And you're going to do it by channeling one of America's greatest writers: Ernest Hemingway.

Hemingway is best known as a writer of spare and tight prose. His contemporary, William Faulkner, once observed that Hemingway "has never been known to use a word that might send a reader to the dictionary." Hemingway had also never been known to take a punch without hitting back, and he said this in response: "Poor Faulkner. Does he really think big emotions come from big words? He thinks I don't know the ten-dollar words. I know them all right. But there are older and simpler and better words, and those are the ones I use."

As proof of Hemingway's ability to pare prose down to the bare essentials, he was once challenged to write a story in six words. The result was this:

For sale.
Baby shoes.
Never worn.

In six words, Hemingway painted a haunting picture of hope turned to despair. He also inspired a cottage industry of six-word storytellers. Here are some of our favorites:

Former third wheel. Now a unicycle.
Found true love; married someone else.
Followed the rules; wish I hadn't.
Unsure, but you would never know.
I'm not walking away, just forward.

Our all-time favorite six-word story ranks right up there with Hemingway's as an exemplar of brevity, power, and passion. It was written to honor Steve Jobs, the visionary leader of Apple, following his death:

iPad, iPod, iPhone, iTouch, iSad, iThankyou.

20/20 Sight Line: The Six-Word *You*

The next step is to create a six-word story about yourself. These are the rules:

- You must use exactly six words.
- You must tell a story or make a definitive statement.
- You must reveal an important aspect of your character.

Here is some inspiration to get you started. These are examples created by some of Phil's students at Boston College:

Clear eyes, full heart, won't lose.
I get the job done, period.
Believing in myself makes me unstoppable.
Living to make an impact locally.
I am a catalyst for change.
Combining traditional values with modern intelligence.
Warming your heart, winning your favor.
I am a human Rubik's Cube.
My deep complexity coincides with simplicity
Pint-sized person. Jam-packed personality.
Born with silver spoon. Want plastic.

This process can be quite intimidating for some, so you may want to start by writing a six-word story about someone else – a celebrity, a close friend, or family member. Once you're ready to write your own story, don't stop at one. We're all many-sided creatures, so explore all the crooks and crannies of your being, your character and your brand.

And here's a final bit of six-word inspiration:

Stop procrastinating your personal brand articulating.

Please visit us at **20-20MindSight.com/chapter18** to download the worksheet, access new content, see how others have completed the exercise, and maybe share your results.

CHAPTER 19: *"WHAT WOULD STEVE DO?"*

Stay True To Yourself

Just like fingerprints, the journey through life is unique for each individual. None of us can successfully take on another person's character, value system, or thought processes as our own. That even goes for Tim Cook, the successor to Apple's legendary leader, Steve Jobs. Cook and other members of Apple's executive team are committed to honoring Jobs' dying request that they never pause to ask, "What would Steve do?" Instead they maintain a singular focus on doing what is best for Apple.

Jobs was an artist in the truest sense of the word; and like all great artists he not only broke the rules, he substantively redefined them. He imagined and delivered products that few of us had even contemplated. He focused on creating products and services that helped people harness the power of technology to make their lives better. He never worried about "maximizing shareholder value," and yet he grew Apple into the largest and most admired company in the world. Why shouldn't his successors try to channel his spirit?

Think about it from this perspective. All of the great artworks housed in the Metropolitan, the Louvre, the *Accademia*, and the world's other great museums can today be digitally replicated down to the tiniest nuance. None of those copies, however, as perfect as they might appear, would be considered art. It's the same way with character and genius. Steve Jobs realized that the rules he redefined would require additional redefining after his death. His successors would inherit a far different world with a different set of rules, obstacles, and opportunities. If Cook and his team tried to manage Apple by looking backward they would be left in the dust of a new crop of hungry competitors. Tim Cook was succeeding an icon who had traveled an iconoclastic path, and he needed to do the same thing as Jobs – except different.

Embrace The Difference

Before reading ahead, please ask yourself this simple Yes-No question: Are you different?

In classes and workshops Phil often poses that question to students and participants and asks them to raise their hands if they consider themselves to be different. In a typical group, less than half usually raise a hand. Phil lets his gaze sweep across the room and, without singling out anyone in particular, he asks the people whose arms remained at their sides or folded in front of them if that means they consider themselves to be the same. Nervous laughter combined with chagrined smiles and raised eyebrows usually ensue and it's all heightened when Phil points out that it has to be one or the other. You're either different or the same.

Phil then repeats the "Are you different" question. Everyone in the room knows they're expected to raise their hands but many of them do so with visible embarrassment and visceral uncertainty. When he first began doing this exercise Phil was surprised and confused by the reaction. Why was it so difficult for people to admit that they were not the same as everyone else? It's common knowledge that even identical twins possess differences in their personalities, worldviews, and even in physical appearance (though you have to look closely). Being different is one of the great blessings of being human and yet we shy away from a simple acknowledgment of that fact. We suggest two reasons for this hesitancy:

- People believe that proclaiming one's "difference" is arrogant and narcissistic – or would be perceived as such by others. They believe different implies better or worse rather than just different. In our politically correct society it's often viewed as ignorant or disrespectful to suggest that men and women are different despite the indisputable differences in physiology and temperament. As the French say, *vive la difference* – especially since the alternative would be a world far too similar to *The Stepford Wives*.

- People don't want to be different. They prefer to blend in with the crowd rather than stand out. Being the same feels safe while it can be downright terrifying to pursue a path different than the masses. Being different can feel like you're building a wall between yourself and others or purposely engendering conflict instead of harmony. Being different entails a risky choice while being the same requires nothing more than blind allegiance to another person or group or to an idea or ideology. Being the same is easy. It's imitation and indoctrination all rolled into one.

This concept came to life when we learned that Tony Bennett had teamed with Lady Gaga to record an album of duets. There are probably no two artists in the history of music that are more different than the always-suave Tony Bennett and the what-will-she-do-next persona of Lady Gaga. And we would bet your life that the devoted fans of both questioned the wisdom of this partnership. Nonetheless, Bennett and Gaga were able to toss aside any preconceived notions and stereotypes. They moved beyond their superficial differences and united in a shared passion to make music that resonated and mattered. They made new fans in the process.

When Tony Bennett was asked about his decision to work with Lady Gaga, he referred back to some advice he'd received at the beginning of his career. He was told to never "imitate another singer, because you'll just be one of the chorus if you do." Today, as a worldwide superstar approaching his ninetieth year, he still takes those words to heart. "It sounds so simple," he says,

"If you just be yourself, you're different than anyone else."

Reject The Culture Of Celebrity

After a recent visit to Yellowstone National Park, Phil can confidently state that the Kardashians have a rival for the title of most overrated American celebrity. The culprit is the Old Faithful geyser. It's not that Old Faithful isn't grand; it's just that it pales in comparison to Yellowstone's many other wonders. Most relevantly, it's a sorry counterpart to the far less celebrated Lone Star Geyser located just three miles away.

We would wager that 99% of first-time visitors to Yellowstone include Old Faithful on their must-see list. They check and double-check the eruption schedule to ensure they arrive shortly before "show time" and then scurry away immediately thereafter. Along the way, of course, they must first search to secure a parking space in one of several adjacent lots (by far the largest in the park) and then clamber for a prime viewing spot among the hordes on the concrete sidewalk that encircles the geyser. Then the eruption begins. Then it ends. In human terms, it ain't got staying power. It's the one-minute man of geysers. So sure, it might be faithful; but that's like saying Charles Manson and Jeffrey Dahmer were nice to dogs.

Then we come to the Lone Star Geyser which you've probably never heard of before. Lone Star is far more impressive than Old Faithful even when it's not erupting. While both are considered cone-type geysers, Old Faithful is a stubby mound compared to Lone Star's towering majesty. But no one visits either geyser for its dormant beauty. It's all about the eruption, and that's where Lone Star kicks some serious ass. From start to finish, Lone Star erupts for a full thirty minutes. Unlike Old Faithful's one-trick-pony quickie eruption, Lone Star delivers two or three minor eruptions and concludes with a massive crescendo. Going back to the human analogy, Lone Star doesn't neglect foreplay but rather builds anticipation to the bursting point and then delivers a climax during which the earth quite literally moves.

So why is Old Faithful so popular and Lone Star is, at best, an afterthought and, at worst, an unknown? Convenience. Old Faithful sits about a football field away from its parking lots, while Lone Star requires a two-and-a-half mile hike to witness its treasures. Viewing Old Faithful is a checkmark on a to-do list, and Phil has to confess that he did check it off his own list. Then he hiked to Lone Star. The geyser sits in the glory of Yellowstone's backcountry and there are no man-made walkways or fences surrounding it. It's all natural. When Phil visited Lone Star and watched its eruption the only other people present were his wife and two other couples. Six people compared to the hundreds he encountered at Old Faithful.

It's a sad yet bizarrely commonplace occurrence.

Many of us consult *The New York Times* bestseller list to decide what to buy or borrow from the library. We pay hundreds of dollars to see Blake Shelton or Rihanna perform while the songwriters who penned their gold records remain nameless because they don't have the right "look" or style. And we pay $12 a ticket to see plotless and witless movies starring "bankable" actors and actresses while ignoring powerful documentaries like *Blackfish* and searing indies like *Fruitvale Station*.

It's easy and convenient to follow the celebrity-worshipping crowd, but it's almost always more valuable and memorable to chart your own understated, iconoclastic path. Is there an Old Faithful in your life that prevents you from experiencing a Lone Star? Are you too focused on the style and marketing of a Kim Kardashian to appreciate the substance and genuine beauty of a Maggie Gyllenhaal?

Jillian and Phil sometimes make that mistake, and we suspect you do as well. Starting today let's all promise to focus on character and depth rather than personality and celebrity.

Argue With Yourself And Make Sure You Win

In his classic book *The Five Temptations of a CEO*, management consultant Patrick Lencioni argues that most corporate executives nurture cultures of harmony rather than conflict. They prefer quiet assent to contentious dissent. Lencioni demonstrates convincingly that effective executives are those that encourage active and constructive discussion and dissension. Unless all opinions are on the table, alternative approaches are never explored and strategic decisions are likely to be the product of lazy groupthink.

The same is true within our own hearts and minds. The key difference is that instead of ignoring the protestations of others we're dismissing the objections and concerns being raised by our very own selves. We all have little voices in the back of our consciousness posing questions we won't voice aloud. The answers to those questions might make us uncomfortable, might force major changes in our lives, and might even refute many of our beliefs and actions to date. The danger in not answering those questions, however, is a life's journey not of your own making and a personal legacy that will come up short of your true potential.

The bottom line result of an iconoclastic approach to your life's journey is steadfast adherence to the belief expressed by Ralph Waldo Emerson:

> *"To be yourself in a world that is constantly*
> *trying to make you something else is*
> *the greatest accomplishment."*

20/20 Sight Line: Hear The Voices

More homework. Think about those little voices in the back of your consciousness. What questions are they asking that make you cringe? Do you have answers that you're afraid to state aloud? We've found that writing down your answers is a good alternative for many people. It forces you to choose the correct words, allows you to edit as you write to achieve maximum precision, and encourages you to keep working at it until the question is fully answered.

So grab a sheet of paper or open a new document on your laptop/tablet/phone. Start with the question that has been challenging you longest or the one that seems most important to your current situation. Write away. You don't need to share it with anyone else. It's for your eyes only – and it will help you visualize your innermost self.

Please visit us at **20-20MindSight.com/chapter19** to download the worksheet, access new content, see how others have completed the exercise, and maybe share your results.

CHAPTER 20: *"NOBODY WANTS TO DIE"*
Live Your Eulogy

Remember the last funeral you attended? Remember how the eulogist marveled about the deceased being a whiz at multi-layered spreadsheets or how her Machiavellian shrewdness helped rocket her up the corporate ladder? Remember how you laughed at anecdotes describing how the deceased was always available for a business call even while coaching his son's little league team or how she'd always put aside personal time to travel across the country to meet with a client?

It never happens. Eulogies focus on the things that made the deceased's life meaningful. In a June 2013 op-ed for *The New York Times*, David Brooks distinguished between the achievements noted on resumes and those highlighted in eulogies. He wrote, "Eulogies aren't résumés. They describe the person's care, wisdom, truthfulness and courage. They describe the million little moral judgments that emanate from that inner region."

You'd be hard pressed to find anyone to disagree with Brooks' statement, yet you'd find it equally difficult to find people who genuinely focus more on the big picture of life rather than the day-to-day rat race of material success. The here and now is easier to deal with than the hereafter – so much so that many people simply ignore the inevitability of death.

Joe Louis famously said, "Everybody wants to go to heaven but nobody wants to die." Louis' quote offers insight on many levels, but it speaks most directly to the fear of death that pervades modern society. In truth the contemporary view of death goes far beyond fear – it's more of a cultural anathema. The word that should never be voiced aloud. The fate that should be avoided – or at least deferred – for as long as possible and at all costs.

Death and the natural progression of aging used to be taken for granted. People's skin wrinkled, their hair turned gray, and their muscles and bones weakened. The elderly and infirm usually died at home witnessed by family and friends. Aging and dying were not hidden from view and were not considered an embarrassment. Facelifts and tummy tucks were only for the rich and narcissistic. When it was time to go, it was time to go. Now when it's time to go, it's time for modern medicine to do its magic. We spare no expense to keep Alzheimer-addled brains alive in pain-racked bodies being spoon-fed while slouched in front of televisions. Evidently life is how you define it.

And how you define life will define how you look at and think about death.

YODO

"You only live once" has become the mantra of the millennial generation. It's a fun-loving maxim with an existential ring that speaks directly to the heart. Ironically, however, it has absolutely nothing to do with the inevitability of death. So starting today, we're going to remind every YOLO-advocating young'un that YODO – "you only die once" – is not just a universal truth, it's also a far more useful roadmap for the kind of journey we want our lives to take.

The Roman philosopher Seneca, who we've quoted elsewhere in the book, wrote an eloquent paean to YODOism:

> You are living as if destined to live for ever; your own frailty never occurs to you; you don't notice how much time has already passed, but squander it as though you had a full and overflowing supply — though all the while that very day which you are devoting to somebody or something may be your last. You act like mortals in all that you fear, and like immortals in all that you desire...

Living each day to its fullest is essential to both YOLO and YODO advocates. Every day is important. Our lives are measured and defined by how

147

we spend our days, the relationships we build, and the value we add to our family and community. But we never know how many days our lives will actually include. Most everyone has experienced firsthand a tragedy of a young life cut short by illness or accident. Most of us hold painful memories of having lost a final chance to tell a loved one how important they were to our lives.

Please reread that last sentence. Why do so many people lose "final chances" to express love and gratitude? Why do final chances even exist? Life is chock-full of opportunities to voice love and appreciation. There is no reason that love and gratitude can only be expressed once. No one gets tired of hearing "I love you" or "you taught me so much" or "knowing you has helped me become the person I am." Opportunities abound for appreciative words – words that are far too important to be left to deathbed confessions. Nonetheless, far too many people have gone to their death from accidents or heart attacks and never had the luxury and joy of having that final chance to hear or say "I love you with all my heart."

"Life is chock-full of opportunities to voice love and appreciation."

From this day forth, acknowledge the people that are important to you. Let them feel your love, gratitude, and respect. Make it a daily habit. Put aside ten minutes a day to write a note or make a phone call to someone special. Share a memory, story or old photograph. And do it "just because." There is no downside to expressing appreciation. You'll feel good and the other party will feel good – and more likely than not, they'll pay it forward.

This poem by the Mexican writer Ana Ma. Rabathe perfectly expresses the YODO concept.

In Life Brother, In Life.
If you would like to make someone you love happy, tell them today.
   In life brother, in life.
If you want to give someone a flower, don't wait until they die. Send it today with love.
   In life brother, in life.

Don't wait to show someone you live them until they die. Tell them today.
    In life brother, in life.
You will always be happy, if you learn to make those around you happy.
    In life brother, in life.
Don't visit cemeteries, nor fill tombs with flowers.
    Instead, fill hearts with love.
    In life brother, in life.

Spent Days = Spent Lives

In her lyrical *The Writing Life*, Annie Dillard states, "How we spend our days is, of course, how we spend our lives. What we do with this hour, and that one, is what we are doing." The question that begs to be answered is whether what we're doing with this hour and the next is what we want to be doing, what we enjoy doing, and what we will remember doing. Think back to yesterday or last week. What do you remember? Was any of it meaningful or satisfying? Why or why not?

Everyone reading this book is going to die, but none of us know precisely when that will happen. But what if you did know? What if you knew you only had one day to live, one week, or one month? What would you do? Would you spend your remaining hours differently? Then when you've determined how you would spend your remaining time on earth, ask yourself why you're not doing that right now.

This is not intended to be a pie-in-the-sky exercise. We're not suggesting that you quit your job and sell your house to travel the world. Rather we'd ask you to consider the things that give you the most pleasure and provide the most satisfaction in your daily life. Things like eating home-cooked meals at the kitchen table with your family, hiking with your dogs, Skyping with your college roommate, painting, gardening, slurping ice cream, playing catch with a grandchild, learning a new language, and a million other things that you find impossible to do without smiling. These are things you can slip into every single day. Yes you may have a tedious job and a horrible commute, but you can make the rest of your time serve as a contributory affirmation of Dillard's observation that this is "how we spend our lives."

> *"How we spend our days is, of course,*
> *how we spend our lives."*

20/20 Sight Line: What Will They Say?

As your final 20/20 assignment, we challenge you to write the eulogy you hope would be spoken at your funeral.

It's inevitable that you're going to die. It's totally out of your control. What is in your control is how people will remember you and honor your personal legacy. This exercise will help focus your remaining time on building out a legacy of love, service, and respect and living a life of empowerment and fulfillment. That, after all, is truly what life and this book are all about.

Here are some ideas to think about to help get you started:

- Who are the people you influenced – and how?
- How are the world, your community, your friends, colleagues, and family better off because of you?
- How did you make a difference that will outlive your mortal life?
- What would people say they most loved and admired about you?
- What will people most miss about you?

In addition to these prompts, we're including the text of Senator Ted Kennedy's eulogy for his slain brother Robert F. Kennedy. Please note that Ted never mentions a word about Bobby's education or career achievements. It's all about Bobby's character, his values, and his impact on the world and those around him.

> *On behalf of Mrs. Robert Kennedy, her children and the parents and sisters of Robert Kennedy, I want to express what we feel to those who mourn with us today in this cathedral and around the world. We loved him as a brother and father and son. From his parents, and from his older brothers and sisters – Joe, Kathleen and Jack – he received inspiration which he passed on to all of us. He gave us strength in time of trouble, wisdom in time of uncertainty, and sharing in time of happiness. He was always by our side.*

Love is not an easy feeling to put into words. Nor is loyalty, or trust or joy. But he was all of these. He loved life completely and lived it intensely.

A few years back, Robert Kennedy wrote some words about his own father and they expressed the way we in his family feel about him. He said of what his father meant to him: "What it really all adds up to is love – not love as it is described with such facility in popular magazines, but the kind of love that is affection and respect, order, encouragement, and support. Our awareness of this was an incalculable source of strength, and because real love is something unselfish and involves sacrifice and giving, we could not help but profit from it.

"Beneath it all, he has tried to engender a social conscience. There were wrongs which needed attention. There were people who were poor and who needed help. And we have a responsibility to them and to this country. Through no virtues and accomplishments of our own, we have been fortunate enough to be born in the United States under the most comfortable conditions. We, therefore, have a responsibility to others who are less well off."

This is what Robert Kennedy was given. What he leaves us is what he said, what he did and what he stood for.

Our future may lie beyond our vision, but it is not completely beyond our control. It is the shaping impulse of America that neither fate nor nature nor the irresistible tides of history, but the work of our own hands, matched to reason and principle, that will determine our destiny. There is pride in that, even arrogance, but there is also experience and truth. In any event, it is the only way we can live.

This is the way he lived. My brother need not be idealized, or enlarged in death beyond what he was in life, to be remembered simply as a good and decent man, who saw wrong and tried to right it, saw suffering and tried to heal it, saw war and tried to stop it.

Those of us who loved him and who take him to his rest today, pray that what he was to us and what he wished for others will some day come to pass for all the world.

As he said many times, in many parts of this nation, to those he touched and who sought to touch him:

"Some men see things as they are and say why. I dream things that never were and say why not."

Please visit us at **20-20MindSight.com/chapter20** to download the worksheet, access sample eulogies, read personal eulogies shared by others, and maybe share your own.

About the Authors

After 25 years as a marketing executive, Phil left the corporate world to pursue endeavors that were more fulfilling personally and more contributory to society. His focus today is on writing and teaching. Phil writes regularly for the *Huffington Post* and has authored a wide variety of books including:

Phil Fragasso, Novelist & nonfiction author

- *Going Both Ways*, Wild Rose Press, 2016
- *Still Counting*, Wild Rose Press, 2016
- *Walden 3.0*, Erewhon Press, 2011
- *Your Nest Egg Game Plan*, Career Press, 2009
- *Marketing for Rainmakers*, Wiley, 2008
- *Good News/Bad News*, Addison-Wesley, 1980

Phil is an adjunct professor at Boston College where he teaches at both the graduate and undergraduate level. Many of the foundational concepts for *20/20 Mind Sight* derived from Phil's teaching experience and his realization that most people know very little about their core values, beliefs, and aspirations.

Jillian Vorce, CEO of
The Jillian Group, Inc.

For over a decade, Jillian has been helping professionals make connections and attain their business goals. An expert at networking and relationship development, she has the ability to open doors and create opportunities. Jillian's trustworthiness and highly positive energy has inspired senior-level executives and business owners across the nation. In 2003 she founded The Jillian Group, Inc., where she and her team provide idea generation, digital marketing & strategic relationship development services for a number of charities and corporations. Her previous work includes:

- TEDx Talk, "The Lens of Connectivity"
- "9 Steps To Increase Your Professional Network" ebook

57628882R00105

Made in the USA
Charleston, SC
17 June 2016